PLOTT HOUND TALES

Legendary People & Places behind the Breed

BOB PLOTT

Published by The History Press
Charleston, SC
www.historypress.net

Cover images: Large front cover image courtesy Jim Casada; top middle image courtesy GSMNP Archives. *Back*: Top photo courtesy GSMNP Archives.

Unless otherwise noted, all photos are from the author's personal collection.

First published 2017

Manufactured in the United States

ISBN 9781625858368

Library of Congress Control Number: 2017938341

Notice: The information in this book is true and complete to the best of our knowledge. It is offered without guarantee on the part of the author or The History Press. The author and The History Press disclaim all liability in connection with the use of this book.

CONTENTS

ACKNOWLEDGEMENTS

It is impossible to thank and personally mention the hundreds of people who have directly or indirectly affected my writing career and my life. Some of them did so with encouragement and inspiration—both personally as well as through their own incredible work. Others unknowingly inspired me through their lack of support and negativity, as I was stubbornly determined to prove them wrong. But all of them—the good and the bad folks—deserve my sincere thanks, and hopefully you know who you are.

However, a few of the truly *good* folks deserve special mention. First and foremost, George and Elizabeth Ellison. Simply put, I would never have written one book, much less five of them along with hundreds of magazine articles, without their help, guidance and inspiration.

I have been friends with this dynamic husband-and-wife team for more than twenty years, but I was a fan of their work long before that. George is literally responsible for my first publishing contract and gave me a brutal but much-needed course in "Writing 101" while serving as an editor for several of my projects. I never thought for a second that I could write a legitimate book of any kind until George convinced me otherwise. Elizabeth provided the stunning cover art for my first project with a painting of a Plott hound that truly captured the essence of the animal while setting the proper tone for the book.

Moreover, both have provided me with good examples of lives well lived and being true to yourself, your beliefs and your art. I think the world of them, and I remain forever in their debt for being my friends and mentors and for giving me role models to aspire to.

Three other people are also responsible for creating "this writing monster," as George so eloquently described me. I *think* that was a compliment, but I digress. Jon Nesbit was my tenth-grade English teacher and a damn good one. At a time when no one believed in me, not even myself, Jon Nesbit did. Not only did Jon believe in me, but he also forced me, despite my protests, to do better, to try harder and to aspire for more in life. I have never forgotten that, and I hope he never forgets the positive impact he has had on my life.

After I got out of college, I was fortunate to meet and become friends with Lynn Moretz and his late wife, Ann. Lynn was also my boss at two different jobs, one of the best I ever had. But more importantly, he was a good friend and mentor when I needed one the most, as was Ann, who remains the most perfect example of the Christian faith I have ever met. They were the first to encourage me to consider writing a book, and their continual, kind persistence further inspired me to do so.

I was never blessed with biological brothers, but I consider myself fortunate to have several of what I like to call "my brothers from other mothers." In addition to George Ellison and Lynn Moretz, this list includes Lewis Penland, Charlie Brown, David Brewin, David Fox, Ben Cook, Danny Shull, Rick Davis, Raymond Bunn, Aaron Thompson, Bill Gibson, Bill Carter, Mike Pritchard, Daniel Whitener, Billy Chapman, Sam MacMahan, Mark Faust, Mike Crisp and Jeff Crisp.

Some of these guys I see or speak with daily and others I may not talk to for months, but regardless, we are always able to pick up right where we left off as if we had just seen each other yesterday. All are special to me. All of them have always had my back, especially David Fox, whom I have known since the first grade. Others, like Lewis Penland, have become my best friends in recent years, which is probably a good thing, as we are so much alike we'd probably both be in jail had we met in our more formative years.

I have experienced tough times with these men, and not once have they failed me. Only four of them—Jeff and Mike Crisp, Aaron Thompson and Mark Faust—are blood kin to me, but all of them truly epitomize the definition of a brother and friend.

As an only child, I never had sisters either. However, another cousin, Linda Plott Chastain, has not only become like a sister to me, but her research assistance was also invaluable to the completion of this book. I simply could not have done it without her. Thanks, Sis!

Speaking of research, for me, research is one of the most enjoyable things about writing a book or article. Not only do you usually learn something interesting, but you also always meet new people, many of whom become friends. I would be remiss not to thank several of them who played integral roles in the completion of this book, although a few have unfortunately passed on.

Despite the extensive bibliography included here, much of the information in this book was provided firsthand by the people who lived it, by friends and relatives who knew the people profiled personally or else by historians who have studied these people and places closely.

Without the input of the following individuals, this book would never have been written: Charlie Shuler, Eddie Parker, Everette Cable, Lee Woods, Helen Cable Vance, Lula Allen Cable, Anne Ballew, the late Oliver Laws, the late Von Plott, Bud Lyon, the late Hub Plott, Shane Plott, Eugene Walker, Eddie Hoge, Joe Polly, Mrs. Louise Plott, Steve Fielder, Vance Biesecker, John Jackson, Dr. Wayne Battle, George Frizell, Lance Holland, Brad Higgins, the late Granville Calhoun, Tommy Wilcox, Leota Wilcox, Jack Orr, Mattie and Mary Orr, the late John Banks, Marshall McClung, Floyd West, Bobby Smith, Rex Suddreth, the late Dewey Sharp, Jack Edwards, Carol Edwards, Charles Miller, the late Stanley Hicks, the late Ray Hicks, the late Ellis Wolfe, the late Moses Owle, Terrell Finley, Pearly Vereen, Bill Crawford, Major Don Rose, Jim Casada, Don Casada, Wendy Meyers, Ken Wise, Libby Kephart Hargrave, Bill Hart and Ernestine Upchurch.

Some of these individuals were, or still are, close friends. A few are kinfolk, while others I barely know. Yet many of them graciously spent many hours allowing me to interview them. Others answered e-mails, phone calls or letters with responses filled with valuable information or pointed me in the right direction to find it. I intended to do more extensive interviews with several of them, but time did not permit me to do so. I intend to correct that problem soon and ask for your patience—you know who you are.

But of this impressive group of scholars, historians, hunters, woodsmen and woodswomen, I must also add that I have never met more knowledgeable experts pertaining to the Great Smoky Mountains than Don Casada, Ken Wise and Wendy Meyers. Their geographical and cultural knowledge of these mountains and our people is astounding. Anytime I have a question about people or places in the Smokies, they always have the answers, and I thank them sincerely for their invaluable assistance and friendship.

The previously mentioned Danny Shull and his good friend Neil Davis, along with Ben Cook, deserve special thanks for their technical expertise with computers and photos. Being a low-tech redneck of the highest order, I need all the technical help I can get. Thanks again!

In addition to George Ellison, several other notable writers deserve special thanks, not so much for this book as much as for their friendship and stellar advice in other projects. *New York Times* best-selling authors Ron Rash and David Joy both have offered invaluable technical and moral support when I needed it most, and both are great inspirations to me.

Ron and I have much in common, as we are nearly the same age and share a lot of similar life experiences. I only wish that I had a fraction of his talent. Ron has the unique ability to make even the most mundane, simple subjects seem eloquently profound, yet by the same token, he is equally adept at artistically honing the most complicated and complex topics down to their most profound simplicity. He is truly a master at his craft.

So, too, is David Joy. I don't know David that well, and he is much younger than me. But thankfully, David recognized us as kindred spirits and graciously offered his input on another book when I first approached him. Helping a total stranger says a lot about him, especially when he is so incredibly busy—as is Ron. I can never thank them both enough.

Jim Casada and Wayne Caldwell are two other fine writers who graciously have offered me feedback over the years, on other projects and research, as well as the business side of writing. And Jim offered quite a bit of insight into this book as well. Thanks to you both.

The late, great John Parris was my first literary hero and remains an inspiration to me to this day. I was honored to include quotes from many of his books and articles in this publication and several of my other projects as well. The first hardcover book I ever bought was an autographed copy of John Parris's *Mountain Bred*. I paid about six bucks for it in 1968 at Bennett's Drug Store in downtown Bryson City when I was eleven years old. The book remains in my library today, along with all of Parris's other great books.

Until that time, it had never occurred to me that anyone could make a living doing exactly what they loved. I am eternally grateful to John Parris not only for his wonderful books and columns but also for that stunning revelation to which I still aspire today.

These writers are all artists of the highest caliber. So, too, are some of my musical friends. Most notably the wonderful band Mountain Faith of Sylva, North Carolina, whose members have been exceedingly kind to my family and me. Longtime friends and stellar musicians Willard Gayheart, Scott Freeman, Dori Freeman, William Ritter and Darren Nicholson, and all the boys in Balsam Range, are other artists who inspire me to further hone my skills. But most of all, they are darn nice folks!

Special thanks go to the Arcadia Publishing/The History Press group for the publication of this project, as well as my previous four books. This is the first time I have worked with commissioning editor Banks Smithers and copy editor Ryan Finn. It was an absolute pleasure. Thanks, Banks and Ryan!

I have saved the best for last. You can't pick your family, and I sure lucked up when I was born into the Plott clan. How many families have their own breed of dog named for them? How cool is that? These amazing people and canines have left me with some big shoes to fill. While I will surely never do so, I am honored to give it my best shot in perpetuating our storied legacy.

I was blessed to have the world's best parents: Mary Thompson Plott and the late Glenn "Big Shine" Plott. What incredible role models they were and always will be to me. I love them dearly and still miss my father daily.

I was further blessed with the planet's best aunt and uncle—the late Cecil and Mildred Plott—who were like my grandparents. Their children and grandchildren were like my brothers and sisters, and I love and thank them all for their support.

You can, however, pick your spouse, and I hit the jackpot there as well. A man could never have a better wife than Janice Brewer Plott or a better son than Jacob Morgan Plott. I am incredibly blessed, and I love you both more than you will ever know. None of my books, programs or honors would have happened without your support—nor, more importantly, would my dogs always get fed. Simple thanks are woefully inadequate, but they must suffice for now.

I fully intended for the acknowledgement section to be brief, but I failed miserably. I apologize for that. However, I must offer one final closing comment. I once asked George Ellison what I should write a book about—or anything else, for that matter. George smiled and simply answered, "Write about what you know and what you are passionate about. Everything else will take care of itself." George was exactly right, and that's precisely what I have tried to do.

BOB PLOTT
December 2016

INTRODUCTION

Most Plott dog enthusiasts—particularly those who have read my previous books—will agree that the Plott hound was given its name for good reason. Family members such as Johannes George Plott and his descendants, most notably Henry, Montraville, Von, Sam, Hub, John and Little George Plott—along with friends such as Taylor Crockett, Gola Ferguson and Isaiah Kidd—were all instrumental in originating and refining the Plott breed. All have been featured in previous books, articles and programs.

However, without the help and contributions of other people and families *not* named Plott, the truth is that the Plott hound would never have received the worldwide notoriety that it enjoys today. It would likely have remained a mostly regional phenomenon.

Many of these illustrious southern mountain families such as the Denton, Rich, Calhoun and Lovin clans, along with renowned individuals like Mark Cathey and Wiley Oakley, among scores of others, played integral roles in the development of the Plott breed and have been profiled in my earlier work as well.

But there are legions of others equally worthy of mention for the major roles they played—and, in some cases, still play—in perpetuating the legacy of the Plott hound. That, in a nutshell, is the purpose of this book. We want to recognize some lesser-known people and places that have contributed greatly to Plott breed history. Again, none of these folks were blood kin to the Plott family. They had no clan obligations requiring them to carry the family torch—they did it strictly due to their passion for the breed and the sport of hunting.

I found it intriguing that almost all the characters in this book lived in or around the Hazel Creek Watershed and hunted there often or else had some other direct ties to the region, the Plott family or the southern Appalachian range. The significance of the Hazel Creek region, hunting clubs and, indeed, the Great Smoky Mountains and its inhabitants are all integral parts of Plott breed history.

Some may question the inclusion of two individuals who, by any conventional societal standard, would be considered outlaws. I make no apologies for that, nor by the same token do I endorse that sort of behavior. But Quill Rose and Andy Orr were indeed a part of our history, and I would add that their notoriety, along with their commitment to the Plott hound, helped bring the breed additional national exposure and respect.

Others might find fault at the inclusion of Jack Edwards, who was only personally involved with the breed for about twenty years. Nevertheless, those two decades were of critical importance to breed history, and Jack has answered historical questions and offered specific insights that would have been forever lost without him. Reliable information of this sort is priceless, and that alone warrants his profile.

Critics may also challenge including the profile of a breed icon who never lived long in the southern Appalachians. It is a valid point, but Frank Methven was born in Kentucky, and his roots run deep in the region. Moreover, no one can question his lifelong dedication to promoting the Plott breed. Frank Methven was simply the best breed ambassador the Plott breed has ever had.

Not only did these people and places help bring worldwide notoriety to the Plott breed, but the inclusion of these individuals also offers further proof of the wildly diverse backgrounds of Plott hound enthusiasts. So, too, does the magnificent land and places that helped mold their unique personalities while further enhancing their personal legends—and that of their dogs.

From outlaws to lawmen, from lawyers and celebrities to farmers, preachers, common folks and everything in between, these Plott legends and places are all rich slices of pure Americana. Regardless of their backgrounds or locations, they all have two things in common: a passion for the Plott breed and a wonderful and colorful story. To me, that is what makes these people, dogs and places truly special, and it is why Plott dogs and Plott people are truly a breed apart from all others.

CHAPTER 1
QUILL ROSE

"An Original Genius"

Much has been written about Quill Rose, and rightfully so. Everything about the man—starting with his unusual name, Aquila Lian Rose—was larger than life. Stories vary as to the origination of his moniker. Some say that Quill's parents, Nathan and Rebecca Rose, named the fourth of their sixth children after the Latin word for "eagle." Others maintain that his name was derived from a biblical character from the New Testament Book of Acts.

No one knows for sure, but considering that Rebecca and Nathan were both strong advocates of education, insisting that all their children could read and write, and since Quill's brother, Jake Rose, later named his own son Eagle, after his beloved sibling, it seems likely that Aquila "Quill" Rose's name came from the Latin connotation.

Regardless, Rose's full name was soon shortened to Quill, and it proved to be a perfect handle for such a colorful and legendary character. His notoriety as a bootlegger and gunfighter are both well documented. But Quill Rose was also one of the earliest documented advocates of the Plott hound breed, and he played a little-known but integral part in Plott breed history.

However, to fully comprehend how Rose brought notoriety to the breed, one must understand all the many other things for which he became famous, starting with his colorful origins and his incredible life story. Quill Rose was born in Blount County, Tennessee, on May 4, 1841, but moved with his family to Cherokee County, North Carolina, in 1849. The youngster found the hills and hollows of Western North Carolina to his immediate liking. Quill took to the mountains like a duck on a June bug.

Although many of the Cherokee tribe had been forced from their native homes by the U.S. government on the infamous Trail of Tears in 1838–39, this remained a remote, dangerous region in the 1840s, marked only on some maps as uncharted "Indian Territory." It was a rugged land filled with abundant game, sparkling streams, few people and ample opportunities to hunt, fish and run hunting dogs. All these things, along with music, quickly became passions for young Quill Rose.

A well-known local fiddler first taught the lad to play the fiddle when he was nine years old. By the age of fifteen, Quill Rose was the star musician at most frontier social gatherings, corn shuckings and church socials. It wasn't long before the teenager began to supply not only the music for these events but also the liquid refreshments for those in attendance. According to Rose family descendant Major Don Rose, Quill had mastered the art of moonshining well before he was out of his teens. Whiskey-making was a Rose family tradition, and Quill learned from the best of the clan, his uncle, John Rose.

By the age of twenty, Quill Rose already had a well-earned reputation in the area as a stellar musician, a crack shot, a hunter without peer, a master moonshiner and a man handy with his fists. Rose also enjoyed training hunting dogs, although it is unknown if he had obtained any Plott dogs of his own by this time.

Over the course of his first two decades on earth, Rose developed close friendships and hunted often with the remaining Cherokee natives still living in the area. He demonstrated an unusual knack for learning languages and quickly became fluent in the Cherokee tongue. The respect Quill gained from his Indian neighbors and his ability to converse with them would serve Rose well during the upcoming Civil War.

His impressive physical stature further complimented his vast array of talents and garnered additional respect for the young man. Rose was a big, handsome fellow, well over six feet tall. Both Horace Kephart, a renowned writer, and Dodette Westfeldt Grinnell, whose family owned a copper mine on Hazel Creek, met Quill later in life and remembered him as being "a splendid looking man, very tall and very likeable."

Journalists Wilbur Zeigler and Ben Grosscup also described Rose as being a "man of fine features and physique, wearing a full dark beard, long black hair and blue eyes." They added that Rose was a good-natured individual "but of desperate character when aroused." Kephart echoed

Quill Rose with scythe. *Courtesy of GSMNP Archives.*

their character assessment, noting that Quill was "usually a friendly and humorous character, despite his undoubted handiness as a gun fighter."

Quill Rose clearly was a likeable and talented individual, although it was equally as apparent that the physically imposing young man was not someone to trifle with. Like many young adults of similar skill sets and dispositions, Rose craved excitement in his life, and he eventually found it as a Confederate soldier serving under Colonel William H. Thomas.

Rose enlisted with Thomas on August 31, 1861, at Qualla Town, near what is now Cherokee, North Carolina. He was later joined by his brothers, Jake and Isaac, who enlisted later that same year. The Rose brothers continued their military training at Thomas's camp in Floyd Bottoms, along the shores of the Oconaluftee River until early 1862. It was not what they expected. Quill was soon bored with the mundane daily activities of military life but managed to retain his sanity by hunting meat for the camp. Rose eagerly anticipated combat, and he didn't have long to wait.

THE CHEROKEE LEGION

It seems somehow fitting that Quill Rose would serve under Colonel William Holland Thomas (1805–1893) during the Civil War. Rose had inadvertently found a commander and military unit that matched his own colorful personality. Thomas, often referred to as "Little Will," was the adopted son of the legendary Cherokee chief Yonaguska and would serve as the first and only white chief of the eastern band of the Cherokee tribe. Thomas was also an attorney, a businessman and a North Carolina state senator during his fascinating life.

But Thomas was best known for his service as chief of the Cherokees and commanding officer of his own military unit during the Civil War. The Thomas Cherokee Legion, also known as the Thomas Legion of Indians and Highlanders, was attached to the Sixty-Ninth North Carolina Regiment of the Confederate army. It was the largest single military unit raised in North Carolina during the war.

As its name implied, it was a unit consisting of white mountaineers and Cherokee tribal members, mostly from Western North Carolina, ranging in size from 1,125 soldiers to more than 2,500 men during the war. At least two of the companies, A and B, were made up entirely of Cherokee warriors, none of whom owned slaves. Rose fit right in with the Cherokees, as the

Left: Colonel Will Thomas, commander of the Cherokee Legion. *Courtesy of North Carolina Archives.*

Below: Thomas Legion reunion of Companies A and B in early 1900s. *Courtesy of North Carolina Archives.*

units consisted of stellar Indian woodsmen and hunters. In just one year, they harvested 540 deer, 78 bears, 18 wolves, 2 panthers and thousands of smaller birds and mammals for fellow tribal members.

Colonel Thomas recognized Quill Rose's skills as a woodsman, as well as his fluency in the Cherokee language. Thus, Quill was assigned to serve as an interpreter and messenger with the Cherokee units and worked closely with both Thomas and Lieutenant John Astoogahtogeh. Lieutenant Astoogahtogeh, a native of Jackson County, North Carolina, was a highly regarded officer. He was once described by a fellow soldier as "a splendid physical specimen and warrior." The young lieutenant was the grandson of Chief Junaluska, a hero of the War of 1812.

While it is true the Legion did not fight at the more famous battles of the Civil War, such as Gettysburg or Bull Run, the unit saw more than its fair share of action while operating almost entirely in east Tennessee and Western North Carolina. Service in these areas was more dangerous than most due to the mixed feelings about the conflict among the local population, as well as the proximity of the Union army in east Tennessee.

Many mountaineers sided with the Union, as few owned slaves. Even the Southern sympathizers fought mostly out of allegiance to their state. Here, more than anywhere else, homes and families were literally divided in their beliefs—some serving with the Union and some with the Confederacy. Conflict between those at home were common, and this problem was further compounded by deserters from both sides who formed roving outlaw bands. These brigands operated under the pretense of their respective beliefs, but whether representing the North or South, they were typically nothing more than cowardly criminals.

The Legion was fighting a battle on two fronts: against these local bushwhackers and against well-trained and usually better armed Union army forces. If Quill Rose was looking for excitement, he had finally arrived at the right place.

Reports on Rose's specific war service vary, but it's clear that he saw plenty of combat. Rose fought in Powell Valley, Tennessee, at the Battle of Baptist Gap on September 15, 1862. Fighting was fierce, and the beloved leader of Rose's unit, Lieutenant John Astoogahtogeh, was killed leading the charge that repelled Union forces. The Cherokee troops were enraged to learn of their leader's death, and several of them scalped dead Union soldiers in retaliation.

Colonel Thomas could not condone these actions and ordered that the scalps be returned to their corpses for burial. Quill Rose reportedly oversaw this task. The publicity received from the scalping sent fear through Union ranks, and Thomas took full advantage of it among his own soldiers as well.

His Confederate troops were issued orders that the Cherokee warriors would be encouraged to scalp all deserters.

Subsequent battles soon followed. Rose saw action at Limestone Station, Tennessee, on September 8, 1863. Lieutenant Colonel M.A. Haynes praised Rose and his men, saying that "the N.C. boys made the charge and the enemy fled before them." Another officer noted, "It was a stubborn fight, lasting over two hours." The Legion captured 290 Yankees, wounded 30 and killed 20, while losing only 6 of their own men.

Rose followed that fight with a losing skirmish at the Battle of Blue Springs, Tennessee, on October 10, 1863. About fifteen thousand Union soldiers defeated fewer than three thousand Confederates. Rebel losses were listed as 220 killed, while Union forces lost 100 men. Outnumbered four to one, the Confederate forces put up a valiant fight. Confederate general John S. Williams specifically praised the Legion and noted, "I have never seen such an exhibition of valor and soldierly bearing."

In addition to serving bravely in these conflicts and at the Battle of Telford's Station, Rose and his men often served as guards for important railroad bridges, supply lines and the Alum Cave, a source for gunpowder production in the Great Smokies. In addition, they rounded up deserters and fought local outlaw militia groups. Rose saw heavy action tracking deserters and skirmishing in Madison County, North Carolina—an area so well known for violence that it was commonly referred to as "Bloody Madison."

Already an excellent marksman and fighter, Rose's action in the Civil War further honed his combative skills. He was good at the job, but by 1864, Quill could see the handwriting on the wall. He was ready to go home and resume his life as a hunter, fiddler and bootlegger. Rose gratefully accepted an honorable discharge from Colonel Will Thomas as the Legion broke winter camp at Ela, North Carolina, in the early spring of 1864.

Sources indicate that Quill Rose was highly regarded by Colonel Thomas, so much so that before Quill's departure, his commanding officer gifted Rose with a brace of Remington pistols, along with allowing Rose to keep a .44-caliber Henry Arms lever-action repeating rifle that Quill had captured from a Yankee during the fight at Telford's Station. He would utilize the weapons well the rest of his life.

But the Civil War wasn't over for Quill Rose. Tensions remained high on the homefront. Rose was forced to fight off fifteen deserters who attacked him shortly after he returned home. It is not known how many of his assailants were killed or injured, but Rose survived unharmed and supposedly added a notch or two to the body count totals he recorded on the grips of his pistols.

LIFE AFTER THE WAR

Aside from that unfortunate incident, Quill Rose returned home a man on a mission. He soon had his liquor still operational and planted some crops, all the while hunting hard and often. His primary objective in life was "to never get catched" selling his illegal wares. Eventually, Quill would even designate a brand name for his spirits: Tanglefoot. Rose's potent liquor was so named because a man could only drink a small amount of it without his feet "getting tangled up."

Rose fiercely opposed the idea that whiskey improved with age. When asked his opinion on the topic, Rose stated, "I kept some for a week one time and I could not tell it was one bit different than when it was fresh and new. My whiskey is as pure as the morning dew." A local judge was one of Quill's biggest customers and once proclaimed that Quill's moonshine was "the best ever made by any man!"

Business was good for the Civil War veteran, but there was one thing missing in his life: a wife. Rose solved that problem when he married Lavica Emeline Hyde in 1867. Better known as Vicey—or, later, Aunt Vicey—Ms. Hyde was raised in nearby Swain County at the head of Forney Creek.

Vicey was of Cherokee descent; some reports say she was a full-blooded Indian, while others maintain she was half Cherokee. Either way, in some circles this sort of mixed-race marriage was frowned upon in those days. Quill, always his own man, cared little for the so-called conventional customs of society. He loved Vicey more than life itself, and heaven help the person who insulted her. It was a near perfect marriage for both.

The young couple purchased land at the head of Wolf Creek in Graham County, North Carolina, and built their first home there. Hunting was better than ever, the soil was fertile and his whiskey business continued to flourish. Reports differ on the exact costs of Tanglefoot. Writers Wilbur Ziegler and Ben Grosscup quoted the price at one dollar a gallon, while others say it was two dollars a quart.

Regardless, Rose's profit margins were significant. Also, the State of North Carolina offered a five-dollar-per-hide bounty on wolves until 1891 that he took full advantage of, and he further supplemented his income by later working as a timber cruiser and blacksmith for Montvale Lumber Company.

Rose made frequent trips to Charleston, North Carolina—now Bryson City—to deliver liquor, collect on wolf bounties and pick up supplies. In April 1868, Rose was confronted by an angry local citizen who demanded that Quill sell him some whiskey. Rose refused and a fight ensued. Quill was shot and seriously wounded in the fray, but he killed his assailant, Bert Rhodes, with a Bowie knife.

After recuperating briefly from his gunshot wound, Rose left the area to avoid being arrested and prevent feuding with his attacker's family, who sought to avenge their deceased relative. It is unclear exactly what transpired over the next twenty-four months.

Some reports indicate that Quill and Vicey left the mountains entirely and relocated to Texas, where they lived for at least two years. Others maintain that they only went as far as Cades Cove and hid out with family members there, while yet another version is that the couple moved in with Vicey's family on Forney Creek.

Quill is rumored to have killed at least one other man during his time in exile. The story goes that a local bully was abusive to his family. Rose warned the rascal to stop the abuse or face the consequences. The man refused and angrily pulled a pistol on Quill. Without hesitation, Rose calmly shot his attacker and added yet another notch to his guns.

There are also stories that the Rhodes clan ransacked the Rose family farm on Wolf Creek and burned it to the ground while Quill and Vicey were in hiding. This apparently satisfied the bloodlust of the Rhodes kinfolk, and things were considered even.

Despite these many rumors, all we know for certain is that Rose killed Bert Rhodes in self-defense and thus avoided criminal prosecution. We also know that Rose and Vicey left their home for almost two years after the incident and that they were living back in Western North Carolina possibly as early as 1869 but certainly no later than 1870. However, all these stories—mythical or factual—only served to further embellish the reputation of Quill Rose as a fighter and blockader.

Eagle Creek

Records show that in 1870, Rose bought 120 acres of land deep in the Great Smoky Mountains, high up on Eagle Creek, near the Tennessee/North Carolina border. Quill and Vicey built a home there and were soon joined by Quill's brother Jake Rose and his family, who constructed a cabin of their own nearby. It wasn't long before the Rose brothers had their whiskey operation back at full capacity.

Quill found the Eagle Creek area ideal for blockading and hunting. Wildlife was abundant, and with his house almost directly on the boundary of two states, he could easily avoid lawmen from either state by escaping into the other. Best of all, the remote property could only be accessed by foot or horseback along a narrow, steep path at least five miles from the nearest wagon road. There was only one way in and one way out. And some lawmen learned that the hard way.

Seymour Calhoun, son of the legendary Granville Calhoun—who was profiled in my second book and is mentioned prominently in this publication—told of the time some revenuers managed to sneak up on Quill at his cabin and place him under arrest.

Quill reminded the officers that he would gladly comply, but in doing so, they would have to pass right by his brother Jake's home on the way out and would surely be killed by Jake and other friends in the process. Quill then offered the lawmen the alternative option of buying some of his homebrew for their return trip and leaving peacefully and safely or else facing the fatal consequences of arresting him. It was their choice. The officers took a moment to review their options before wisely deciding to purchase some Tanglefoot and head safely back home.

In the late 1800s and early 1900s, Rose additionally supplemented his income by doing blacksmith work at his home and at some of the local lumber camps. Over the years, he had become a skilled metalworker, and his work was highly coveted. Quill also had a very unusual blacksmith shop. How that came about is a story worth telling, as well as the tale of the man partly responsible for it.

Legend has it that Rose first met J.E. "Jack" Coburn in the late 1880s. Coburn, a Michigan native, had come south to make his fortune as a timber agent and was known to be a very likable fellow with a wry sense of humor.

A lanky, muscular redhead who wore a bushy mustache, Jack stayed constantly on the move as he traveled throughout the mountains acquiring property and building a financial empire. Coburn made these trips astride his horse, Button, usually with a smile on his face and an unlit cigar perpetually clinched between his teeth. Jack is said to have lit his stogies only once a year—on Christmas Day. He was every bit the character as Quill Rose. Their meeting, and subsequent lifelong friendship, would prove to be fortuitous for Rose.

Being cut from similar cloth, Coburn and Quill immediately formed a bond. Rose, along with most locals, were impressed with Coburn's skill as a fighter. As Coburn was a highly trained boxer, Horace Kephart once called

Jack Coburn riding his horse, Button. *Courtesy of WCU Archives.*

him "a practiced knocker" and added that mountain folk had never seen anyone trained in the pugilistic art of the sweet science, which they referred to as "knock fighting."

After handily dispatching several local toughs, Coburn soon earned the respect of Rose and others, who deemed Jack "a master in the knock fight." Coburn further enhanced his reputation as a pugilist when he later knocked out a man in a Waynesville, North Carolina courtroom who had questioned his integrity.

These attributes made Jack Coburn a local favorite. But more than anything it was Coburn's magnetic personality, his sense of honor and his willingness to help others that enamored him to the locals. Longtime friend Dodette Westfieldt Grinnell said that Jack was "a great and beloved man in Swain County, who loved the Great Smoky Mountains and their people." Few mountaineers loved Coburn more than Quill Rose.

Upon his first visit to Quill's forge, Coburn immediately identified the source of a problem. Keeping the fire properly fanned while forging steel was difficult. Jack supposedly helped the mountaineer engineer a water wheel to power the bellows of the Rose Forge, making it much more efficient and easy to run. It was the first, and perhaps only, forge in the region with bellows

Quill Rose playing a fiddle at his home on Eagle Creek. *Courtesy of WCU Archives.*

powered by a water wheel. Quill was forever in his debt, and that tab would increase in upcoming years.

Although clearly industrious, Rose was a carefree fellow who enjoyed the simple pleasures in life. He often rode a white mule to visit friends or travel to town, and it was not uncommon for him to have his fiddle with him, singing raucously at the top of his lungs, sawing off fiddle tunes as he rode along, with a Plott hound or two trailing happily behind.

Rose's love for the Plott breed is often lost among all the wonderful stories regarding his music and keen sense of humor, along with his moonshining, fighting and metalworking skills. We don't know exactly where or when Quill Rose obtained his first Plott dogs. But considering his location and his lifelong reputation as a hunter and dog trainer, as well as his close association with local renowned hunters and Plott dog people, the list of possible sources is almost endless.

Quill could have easily obtained Plott hounds from the Cable clan, the Calhoun family or from Doc Jones. He may have gotten them from a fellow Civil War veteran such as John Denton, or he could have been one of the many mountaineers who made the trip over to Plott Valley to trade dogs with Mont Plott. We will never know for sure, but we do know that Rose was renowned for his great hunting dogs.

Authors Zeigler and Grosscup first met Rose in 1883 while Quill was still in his prime, only in his early forties. As they approached the Rose homestead, several Plott hounds and curs emerged from around the house barking fiercely in protection of their masters. Quill came out on the porch and called off his dogs before asking the strangers to express their intentions: "If you are hunters or gentlemen—then you are welcome, but if you are revenuers or a sheriff's posse then be gone!"

After establishing they weren't lawmen, the scribes were invited to a hearty dinner in the Rose home. Quill warmed to the duo quickly and agreed to take them on a deer hunt. They offered the following interesting observations about Rose's character, his dogs and his skill as a dog handler, as well as Quill's life in the Great Smoky Mountains:

> *Rose and his family are Blockaders, living outside of school districts and state protection. They refuse to pay taxes and are totally self-sufficient, they have no need for state benefits or roads. Rose recognized no formal authority and lives in a pure state of natural liberty, depending only on his own strength and daring, and the seclusion of his home.*

The writers further observed that Quill kept seven hunting dogs at his home. At least three of them were purebred Plott hounds, and the others were mixed-breed curs and Plotts. They found the Plott dogs especially impressive and remembered them as having "keen noses, clear eyes, shapely heads and lithe limbs." Rose and other notable hunters of his era were well known for their well-trained hounds. The visitors noted that

> *their dogs held themselves strictly to their master's orders, and they have reduced dog training to a fine art. Few need to be yoked or leashed, and respond simply to their master's word. When a scent is sprung, one hound will be ordered to leave the pack and follow the trail, with the others to follow, giving each their turn.*

Quill lamented to his guests that for decades he had killed twenty or more bears annually, but that in recent years he only harvested eight to ten bruins. He added that "every man in the Smokies owns dogs now, and game, especially bear and deer, is getting scarce."

He further regaled the scribes with stories of wolf hunting and explained why he carried a mad stone to cure snake bite and rabies. (A mad stone is a white- or blue-colored gallstone occasionally found in the gallbladder of a deer. Many old-time hunters believed that the stones not only were good medicine against snakes and rabid animals but also brought good luck.)

The writers were duly impressed with Quill's dogs and his hound training skills, but they were equally pleased with the multipurpose capabilities of his dogs. Rose noted that his hounds were "prime fighters," fully capable of running bears, deer, wolves or even small game. Hunter, herder, protector and friend—these dogs could do it all.

The journalists concluded their visit to Eagle Creek by participating in a successful deer hunt with Quill and his hounds. But before embarking on the hunt, Rose cheerfully offered his guests "a dram of whiskey," which they gratefully accepted.

The written account of their visit with Rose would prove to be a highlight of Grosscup and Zeigler's 1883 book, *The Heart of the Alleghenies*, and it would be the first large-scale recognition given to Quill Rose and his hounds, although it would not be their last experience in the national spotlight.

Two of Quill's favorite Plott dogs were called Ring and Snap. Quill's wife, Vicey, was particularly fond of them too. The story goes that Quill once planned a day trip into Bryson City for business and decided to take the train from Proctor into town. Ring and Snap followed Rose dutifully to the station before Quill realized that he could not take the hounds aboard the train with him.

Figuring that he would return later in the day, Rose just threw his hat to the ground and ordered his Plott dogs to stay there until he returned. The hounds did as they were told, and Quill boarded the train for town. Unfortunately, Quill sampled a bit too much of his own whiskey while visiting with friends and spent the night in town, oblivious of his loyal canines still waiting back in Proctor. Rose returned home the next morning after catching a wagon ride back to Medlin with a buddy.

Upon his return, Vicey inquired as to where her two favorite dogs were. When she learned that Quill had left them in Proctor, she angrily demanded that he retrieve them immediately. Never one to cross his beloved wife, although undoubtedly hungover, Rose headed back down the mountain to find his dogs. When he arrived at the station later in the day, Quill found Ring and Snap still there, patiently waiting for him, adhering to their master's command as ordered. Rose made sure the dogs were watered before taking them back to Eagle Creek. Vicey surely had a feast waiting for them, as she treated Quill's dogs like the children she never had.

TWILIGHT YEARS

One of the great disappointments of Quill's life was that he and Vicey were never blessed with children of their own. However, their nieces and nephews were beloved by the couple. Quill was especially fond of his three nephews: Eagle, George and Theo.

Unfortunately, George and Theo Rose died violently at a young age. Rose reportedly felt some responsibility for their deaths and was devastated by their passing. His nephews tried to live up to Quill's outlaw image without understanding that their uncle was, by all accounts, a good man who simply made whiskey and defended himself only when needed.

Quill was approaching his twilight years by the time he met the acclaimed writer Horace Kephart. Rose was at least in his mid-sixties by then, but still a strong man and a hard hunter who remained ardently dedicated to the whiskey trade. The author was rightly impressed with the vim and vigor of the iconic blockader, and Kephart would feature Quill prominently in his future work.

Over the next few years, Kephart would become a close friend of Quill's and even joined their mutual friend Jack Coburn in defending Rose when he was finally brought to trial for moonshining at the ripe old age of seventy-two. Father Time had finally caught up with the old moonshiner and bear hunter. After decades of chasing his Plott dogs after bears in the Great Smoky Mountains and running from revenuers, Quill Rose's body was nearly worn out. Quill was rightly concerned that he might be spending the rest of his life in jail if he was convicted by Judge James Boyd.

What Rose didn't know was that his friends Jack Coburn, Horace Kephart and Dr. Foster Sondley—all of whom had accompanied Quill to

Horace Kephart in camp. *Courtesy of GSMNP Archives.*

court—had made a secret plea bargain arrangement with Judge Boyd to acquit Quill, but only if Rose was willing to permanently retire from illegal whiskey production.

Quill knew none of this as he was asked by Judge Boyd, "How do you plead, Mr. Rose, guilty or not guilty?"

Quill paused a moment, carefully pondering his response, before finally answering, "Maybe." The courtroom erupted in laughter before the judge called the court to order. Judge Boyd then dismissed the charges, with the understanding that Rose would never make Tanglefoot again. Thanks to his friends, Quill Rose was a free man, and his liquor making days were done.

While old age might have physically slowed Rose down, it did nothing to dampen his spirit or his love for Vicey. The story goes that Vicey's feelings were hurt badly when she was not invited to a lady's circle meeting in town simply because of her Cherokee heritage. The prim and proper social group was for white women only.

Quill was outraged by this and went to the meeting himself to confront them. When the women admitted that Vicey was not invited because she was a Cherokee, Quill cursed them and told them that they were not fit for the company of his wife. He then urinated in their punch bowl to further emphasize his point. This is yet another classic Quill Rose tale that may or may not be true, but I hope it was.

With the best years of their life behind them, Quill and Vicey sold their home at Eagle Creek to Vicey's nephew for $1,000 in 1918. Quill gave his faithful hunting dogs to family members and made plans to relocate to Cades Cove, Tennessee. The couple lived there with their nieces for the remainder of their lives.

But before he left Eagle Creek, Quill made one last trip to Bryson City to see his friend Jack Coburn. Upon his arrival, with tears in his eyes, Quill gifted Coburn with his treasured pistols, telling his old friend, "I want you to have them, I won't be needing them anymore."

Coburn was shocked yet touched by the gift. He later observed that there were indeed several notches carved in the grips of the old Remington revolvers. Quill bid his friend farewell for good and permanently left town.

Quill Rose died in his sleep at the age of seventy-nine in 1920. He was buried with full military honors, befitting a Confederate veteran, in the family cemetery in Townshend, Tennessee. Vicey would follow him in death two years later. She was buried by his side in 1922.

Horace Kephart once described his friend Quill Rose as "an original genius." That short description succinctly sums up Aquila Lian Rose. Quill

Quill Rose and wife, Vicie, sitting, with nieces standing in rear. *Courtesy of WCU Archives.*

was indeed a one-of-a-kind character, respected even by his enemies as a man of honor who always stayed true to himself.

The word *genius* is also appropriate in describing Quill's totally self-sufficient lifestyle and his ability to do anything well that he set his mind to. Quill Rose lived a life of freedom in the truest sense of the word, yet he was a fiercely dedicated family man. Most anyone can admire that.

Rose would have been a legendary local figure regardless, but his involvement with writers Wilbur Ziegler, Ben Grosscup and Horace

Kephart helped bring worldwide notoriety to himself and the Plott hound breed. Kephart's *Our Southern Highlanders*, which recorded Rose's bear hunting adventures—along with those of Granville Calhoun, Doc Jones, Bill Hyde and the Cable clan—brought extensive exposure to Plott dogs and the sport of bear hunting for well over a century. The book was a bestseller from the day of its initial publication in 1913, and it remains in print still today. Moreover, it further introduced the world to the Plott breed and mountain bear hunting culture. (We will discuss this topic in further detail in chapter 3.)

Outlaw, musician, blacksmith, gunfighter, blockader, soldier, devoted husband, master bear hunter and Plott dog man—Quill Rose was all these things and much more. But above all, he was an American original, and as one of the earliest documented advocates of the Plott hound breed, Quill Rose deserves a permanent position of honor in Plott breed history.

CHAPTER 2

ANDY ORR

"A Desperate and Bad Man"

Major George Plott once said that it takes a special person to own and hunt a purebred Plott hound correctly—or, to be more specific, his exact words were, "The man who isn't game isn't fit to have him."

Plott—better known as "Big George"—was more than qualified to make this statement. The huge former U.S. Cavalry officer knew something about grit and courage. He was a combat veteran of two world wars, World War I and World War II, and fought against Pancho Villa on the Mexican border while serving under General John "Black Jack" Pershing in 1916 and 1917.

Major Plott knew his Plott hounds equally as well, along with what was required to do them justice. A son of Montraville Plott and brother to John, Robert, Sam and Von Plott, Big George was no stranger to bear hunting, and he had raised more than his share of Plott dogs.

Big George's assessment was particularly true in the early days of the Plott breed, before official breed registration. Back then, hunting was often a matter of survival. Gritty mountain hunters had to follow their dogs close to harvest game, and the only way to do so was on foot, keeping the hounds within hearing distance in some of the harshest terrain and most adverse conditions in North America. There were no tracking collars, cellphones or motorized vehicles to make the job easier in those days. Daily hunts covering twenty miles or more per day on foot were routine.

These men were almost superhuman, and their Plott hounds were cut from the same cloth. Many of them were colorful characters to some degree, and all possessed tenacious grit that matched their magnificent dogs. Most were simply solid citizens and good family men who hunted to put food on the table.

However, a few of them were just downright dangerous—men normal folks wisely avoided if possible. The most notable of them was the ferocious but little-known outlaw by the name of Andy Orr, known far and wide as a "desperate and bad man." Andy Orr undoubtedly had the game and grit to match his beloved Plott hounds—or anything else.

A little background on the Orr family is required to set the stage for Andy's remarkable story, as they were, and remain, one of the most renowned hunting clans in southern mountain history. The Orrs were also avid Plott hound enthusiasts—or, in some cases, mixed-breed Plott advocates.

Brothers Dave and George Orr served in the Union army during the Civil War, and they used their mustering out money to buy a large tract of land in the Slick Rock area of Graham County, North Carolina, near Big Fat Gap in about 1867. Some records indicate that the brothers were originally from South Carolina, while others maintain that it was Tennessee. But Graham County was where they would become famous.

At that time, this area was referred to as simply "uncharted Indian Territory." But the rugged mountains surrounding the land soon became known as the Dave Orr Mountains. It was harsh, unforgiving land that required a man to be self-sufficient to survive. However, for folks like the Orr boys, men with the right kind of skill sets—and the right kind of dogs—it proved to be a literal hunting paradise.

Dave and George Orr achieved iconic status as hunters and dog men, and subsequent generations followed suit, meeting or exceeding the high standards of their ancestors. Bart Orr killed fifty-seven bears in his hunting career, the last one when he was eighty-six years old. Other famous Orr family hunters included Jim, Jerry, William, David, "Little" Will, George, Lee, Erskine and Andy Orr. But no story of the Orr family would be complete without first mentioning Andy's cousin, "Little" Will Orr.

"Little" Will Orr was probably the most well known of the hunting Orr clan. He learned his hunting skills from his father, George, and his uncle, Dave Orr. Will once killed thirty-one bears in a single season while hunting the Hazel Creek Watershed and seven boar hogs in only one month in 1946.

Jim Gasque mentioned Orr prominently in his classic 1947 book, *Hunting and Fishing in the Great Smokies.* According to Gasque, Little Will's preferred hunting dog was half purebred Plott hound and half redbone. This cross resulted in an almost solid black dog with brindle trim.

Orr family and their dogs in early 1900s. Andy Orr is on the left, and J.D. Orr is on the right. *Courtesy of Jack Orr.*

Orr also perpetuated the family tradition of moonshining, and he later spent a year in jail for his efforts. But Orr had no regrets and was once quoted as saying, "Making liquor was more profitable and a hell of a lot easier than working behind a plow for ten cents a day." It's probable that Little Will learned his moonshining skills from Uncle Dave Orr or, perhaps, even from Andy Orr.

Regardless, it is a well-known fact that the Orr family and the Birchfield clan were some of the finest hunters and renowned liquor makers in Graham County and beyond. Their rivalry apparently led to at least one murder as well, which leads us to the outlaw Andy Orr.

Andy Orr was the son of Dave and May Medlin Orr. He was born in either 1869 or 1873 (his death certificate says 1873, but other sources are adamant it was 1869) in either east Tennessee or Graham County—more likely the latter. Not much is known of Andy's early life. He grew up hard and quickly developed a well-earned reputation as a hot-tempered man and superb hunter. Orr briefly tried his hand as a coal miner but hated the work. He cared little for logging or farming either, preferring to spend most of his time hunting, fishing and playing music.

Andy was also well known locally for his musical skills as a fiddler. Two Orr relatives—Mattie and Mary Orr—told Graham County historian Marshall McClung and me in 2006 that "Uncle Andy could not read or write nary a lick, but he was a real smart man and an awfully fine fiddle player. That man could play the strings off a fiddle!"

In the late 1800s, Andy Orr married the former Elizabeth "Betsy Jane" Colvin, and they had several children together. Apparently, Mrs. Orr was as hot-tempered as her fierce husband. Local lore maintains that Betsy Jane Orr killed a Cherokee woman in a fit of jealous rage after she suspected the woman of having a relationship with Andy.

With a growing family to support, Orr began to look for a more profitable vocation that allowed him ample time to bear hunt and fish—his true passions in life. Orr eventually found exactly what he was looking for when he entered the liquor business.

Before examining Andy's career as a bootlegger, let's first discuss his love of bear hunting and his dedication to the Plott breed. It is not known where his strain of Plott hounds originated, but it was probably from the Denton or Lovin clans. Unlike some of his kinfolk, Andy favored a purebred, full-blooded Plott hound as opposed to any sort of mixed-breed canines—both the Dentons and Lovins were strong advocates of purebred Plott dogs, and both lived nearby.

Like many mountain hunters, Orr would tolerate no disrespect to either himself or his dogs. Orr is believed to have killed at *least* seven men during his lifetime, and three of them were murdered over arguments about his Plott dogs or someone allegedly mistreating them.

Almost any documented bear hunt between the late 1800s and 1915 finds the name of Andy Orr on the roster. He hunted with southern mountain hunting icons such as Sam Hunnicutt, Mark Cathey, Cub Denton, Dave Swann, Nate Birchfield, Ed Hyatt, Granville Calhoun, Ike Whitson and various members of his own family, including his father, Dave Orr—all of whom had their own fine lines of hunting canines.

Some (like Cub Denton, Sam Lovin, Andy Orr and Mark Cathey) preferred purebred Plott dogs, while others (like Sam Hunnicutt and "Little" Will Orr) favored mixed breeds. Hunnicutt's preference, for example, was a combination of a large purebred beagle and a redbone, while Little Will's was the previously mentioned Plott hound and redbone cross.

But regardless of their dog preferences, Andy and his friends hunted hard, deep and often all over the Smokey Mountains and surrounding ranges as well, including the Deep Creek and Hazel Creek Watersheds, Slick Rock and Big and Little Santeetlah among other locations. They usually had great success in their hunts, though sometimes with strange results.

In 1921, Sam Hunnicutt wrote of a bear hunt in the Unaka Mountains that took place in the early 1900s. The hunt was led by Hunnicutt and Andy Orr and their remarkable dogs—Sam's mixed-breed canines and Andy's purebred Plotts. These old-time hunters had no problem with their multipurpose dogs chasing other game besides bears, as Hunnicutt reported that they killed three bruins but also six coons, two deer and one or two turkeys in the midst of the bear hunt. On at least two occasions, Hunnicutt stated that their dogs and party diverted from pursuit of the bear to kill the coons and two bucks and then returned to the bear trail to bay and harvest a bruin.

Orr and Hunnicutt clearly shared a mutual respect for each other. But with Andy Orr—and to some degree Sam Hunnicutt, too—that admiration

Hunters at clubhouse on Deep Creek in early 1900s, including Sam Hunnicutt (*third from right*), Granville Calhoun (*on porch with hat*) and Mark Cathey (*standing in center with gun on his shoulder*). *Courtesy of Jim Casada.*

only went so far. Legend has it that Andy Orr, Sam Hunnicutt and their respective dogs were returning from a successful bear hunt deep in Graham County when they approached a river crossing on the Little Tennessee River.

The duo had left a john boat hidden in the brush to ferry them back across the stream, but someone had already used it and left it tied on the opposite side. One of them was going to have to swim the icy river to retrieve it, an option even more unappealing in the frigid winter weather. Andy was a well-known hard case, but Hunnicutt was a tough customer too; both expected the other to do the swimming.

Andy resolved the issue when he drew his pistol and aimed it at Sam's head. Orr then ordered Hunnicutt to swim the river and return with the boat. Irate but knowing Andy's reputation as a killer, Sam did as he was told, swam the frigid stream and returned the vessel to Andy.

With his gun still leveled on Sam, they loaded their gear and dogs and prepared for the ferry trip across the river. Just prior to launching, Andy let down his guard, and Sam got the drop on Orr, aiming his own weapon at Andy before disarming him.

A tense standoff developed as both men summed each other up. Hunnicutt ordered Andy to stay put while he crossed the river in the boat. Andy could swim back across and retrieve his gear and dogs—just as Sam had been forced to do. Hunnicutt later said that he felt sure Andy would retaliate. But instead, Andy smiled at Sam and said, "Well, Sam, I didn't know you had it in you." Orr laughed and watched as Hunnicutt got in the boat and headed back to the other side of the stream.

Sam tied up Andy's Plott hounds on the opposite shore and quickly hit the trail. Hunnicutt remained certain that Andy would swim the river and seek retribution. But Andy did nothing of the sort, apparently holding no grudge. He and Sam later laughed about the incident often.

But others weren't so lucky. It was custom among locals that you were obligated to ask an unwanted visitor to leave your property three times before you could legally shoot them for trespassing. If they still refused to leave, they were fair game and could be "paid for," or legally shot by the landowner.

Andy Orr's nieces, Mattie and Mary Orr, said that Andy invoked this rule while in their father's presence and killed an unnamed visitor who thrice refused Andy's warnings to depart. This was Orr's sixth victim—including the three men he had previously murdered over his Plott dogs. The Orr sisters added that even though Andy was their uncle, they were so afraid of him that they would hide under the bed or in a closet whenever he visited.

Orr once came to their homestead near the head of Rock Creek and threatened to kill his own brother—their father—over a dispute pertaining to a bear Andy had trapped. Evidently, his brother had found the dead bear decomposing on Andy's trap line and disposed of it. Andy felt that his sibling had stolen the bear from him and vowed to kill him for his actions. Fortunately, he was talked out of it.

Andy Orr was the great-uncle of Maryville, Tennessee resident Jack D. Orr, who graciously provided me with additional stories about his infamous relative. Jack said that Andy Orr was constantly armed, day or night. His 32-.20 Winchester repeating rifle was like an extension of his right hand. Andy took his meals with the weapon lying across his lap and never went anywhere without the rifle, usually with a brace of pistols as well.

Although a known killer, Orr respected courage—as proven in the Hunnicutt story—and Jack Orr recounted a similar situation with Nathan Hughes in 1916. Andy got in an argument with Nathan Hughes on the Old Tennessee Turnpike. Nathan's son, Johnny Hughes, came to his father's defense and challenged Andy, saying, "You wouldn't have the nerve to talk to my Pa like that if'n I had a gun!"

Orr responded by shifting his rifle from his right to left hand and pulling a pistol from his frock coat. He then tossed the six-shooter to the younger Hughes and ordered him to "have at it!"

Johnny Hughes was as good as his word; he caught the pistol and wasted no time in shooting Andy Orr three times. Despite his injuries, Orr returned fire with his Winchester and severely wounded Hughes in the leg. The gunmen were taken to the hospital in Maryville, Tennessee, for treatment, and ironically, both were placed in the same hospital room to recuperate. Both recovered fully, and there is no evidence of further trouble between the two. Hughes had earned the respect of the outlaw.

Erskine Orr, the father of Jack Orr, often fished with Andy and paddled the boat for him on fishing trips. Erskine stated that a game warden approached them one day and asked to see Andy's fishing license. Andy patted the Winchester rifle lying in his lap and tersely replied, "This is the only license I need. Do you need to see any more of it?" The officer wisely retreated and left the Orr boys alone.

Andy even shot and wounded his own father, Dave Orr, in a dispute at the family homestead. Some reports indicate that the shooting was accidental, while others maintain it was intentional. Andy's brother, James Will Orr, witnessed the incident. He was supposedly the only man Andy feared, and for good reason. James Will Orr was a highly respected deputy sheriff in

North Carolina. Deputy Orr vowed revenge and had to be restrained by several men as Andy escaped to Tennessee. Will followed in close pursuit, but Andy made yet another successful getaway.

In still another incident, a rookie lawman decided that he would build his reputation by arresting Andy Orr for making and selling liquor. Someone tipped Andy that the deputy was coming, and he was ready for him. When the officer arrived at the Orr homestead, he acted under the premise of a private citizen wanting to purchase liquor. Andy questioned his sincerity and expressed doubt that the deputy was a drinking man. The officer insisted that he was indeed looking to buy spirits and gained further confidence as he noticed that Andy's ever-present Winchester rifle was out of reach, propped in a corner.

The deputy's courage soared as he took the opportunity to inform Andy that he was under arrest. Orr acknowledged that his rifle was indeed out of range and wasn't loaded anyway. He then drew his hidden pistol and warned the deputy that his handgun, however, was loaded, as was the second pistol he also produced to increase his firepower.

Orr pointed the weapons at the officer and said, "Now, since you proclaim to be a drinking man, I want you to have a drink with me." Orr chuckled and ordered the officer to drink every drop of a freshly brewed jar of liquor. The deputy attempted to follow Orr's instructions, but he passed out before he could finish the entire quart of potent homebrew. When the deputy finally woke up, he hurriedly returned to the sherriff's office and resigned in embarrassment from his job.

Making and selling liquor was not uncommon in the southern mountains. Men like Quill Rose, Blaine Blevins and Sam Birchfield—among many other notable hunters of the era—all supplemented their income by selling moonshine. Most law-abiding citizens, and sometimes even local law officers, tended to overlook it if the business was relatively discreet and caused no major harm to the community.

Andy Orr readily joined their ranks, but unlike most of his moonshining comrades, he wasn't satisfied with quietly selling small batches of his wares to a limited local market; he had much bigger ideas. Orr formed a sort of mountain mafia, an armed gang of at least five men, including his second in command, Tom Shope, to assist him in his efforts. Together they made large amounts of liquor and then transported their wares to every major logging camp in the region to sell on payday.

Between 1900 and 1916, Orr's illegal enterprise grew to epic proportions, and he made no secret of his intentions. Orr and his gang would ride into the logging camps across the region, and Andy would shamelessly peddle his goods while his heavily armed gang guarded him and prevented any sort of intervention.

By 1915, Orr's notoriety had gained attention statewide. On July 7, 1915, the *Fayetteville Weekly Observer* newspaper noted, "Bootlegging is rampant in western North Carolina logging camps, due mainly to a bad man named Andy Orr. Orr has an armed guard and visits camps every pay day. Orr's gun carries several notches for those who have interfered with his unlawful business. Even bold revenue agents are said to fear him." The *Greensboro Daily News* on August 27, 1915, added, "Andy Orr is a desperate bad man who has murdered many men."

Pless Birchfield became Andy's last murder victim in Graham County in 1916. Birchfield, supposedly a rival moonshiner but perhaps just a concerned citizen, took offense at Andy's murderous exploits and burgeoning illicit enterprise and confronted him about it.

After a heated argument, Orr shot and killed Birchfield, thus adding a seventh notch to his gun. Some reports, however, indicate that Orr's murder total was grossly underestimated and that his kill total was easily in the double digits. Whatever the final tally, Birchfield's murder outraged the citizens of Western North Carolina, and they demanded Orr's capture. Orr escaped to Oklahoma to hide out until things blew over.

Andy enjoyed life in Oklahoma. Despite his fugitive status, he felt relatively safe living in Cherokee Territory, although Orr vowed that he would never be taken alive. Orr was unaware that federal marshals, accompanied by Graham County sheriff Ammons, were traveling to Oklahoma to arrest him. The officers arrived in early 1917 and were either incredibly lucky or had planned their attack wisely, as Orr was captured without a shot while putting a roof on a building. His trusty Winchester and pistols, for once, laid on the ground below him.

The February 5, 1917 edition of the *Asheville Citizen Times* confirmed that Sheriff Ammons of Graham County captured Orr in Oklahoma. The trial was held in Asheville—instead of Graham County—due to concerns that Birchfield relatives would seek their revenge or that Orr's gang, led by Tom Shope, would try to break Andy out of jail.

The hearing went smoothly and without disturbance. In late February 1917, Andy Orr was sentenced to twenty years in the Brushy Mountain State Penitentiary in Morgan County, Tennessee. He remained incarcerated there the remainder of his life. On December 31, 1931, the infamous outlaw Andy Orr died of what his death certificate describes as "heart weakness." He was fifty-eight years old.

Orr's nieces, Mattie and Mary Orr, as well as his great-nephew, Jack Orr, maintain that no one claimed Andy Orr's body and that it was thrown out in the prison garbage heap to be eaten by hogs. The Graham County bad man had lived by the sword and died by it.

Andy Orr's illegal, brutal behavior is inexcusable. Yet his dedication to the Plott breed, his amazing hunting skills and his diverse role in breed history warrants his inclusion as an obscure, yet important, Plott breed legend of the southern Appalachians.

CHAPTER 3

THE BLEVINS AND CABLE CONNECTIONS

Much of Plott hound history is easier to follow than a hot bear track in freshly fallen snow. Other aspects are shrouded in mystery, even controversy. Many of these arguments revolve around the specific origins of the breed or, more frequently, questions regarding infusions or outcrosses from different bloodlines outside the Plott family lineage.

Some famous outcrosses within the Plott hound line have been well documented—such as the breeding of a Lep dog, owned by Georgian Elijah Crowe, with a Plott canine owned by Montraville Plott in the late nineteenth century. Over the course of more than two centuries, there were undoubtedly other outcrosses made outside the family bloodlines as well, although I believe they were rare.

However, there is no doubt that the infusion of the Blevins and Cable dogs into the Plott line were classic examples of two additional early outcrosses made in the late nineteenth and early twentieth centuries. Nor can anyone question the integral role that the Blevins and Cable hounds played in Plott breed history.

Plott icon Gola Ferguson's legendary Boss and Tige perfectly illustrate the Blevins connection. These dogs, both whelped in 1928, had at least one-fourth Blevins bloodlines in their lineage and maybe more. Of the almost one hundred Plott hounds first registered by the United Kennel Club (UKC) in 1946, no fewer than eighty of them had ties back to these two illustrious canines.

Above: Dr. J.F. Abel, *at far left*, in early 1900s photo taken at Haywood Rod and Gun Club. *Courtesy of Charles Miller.*

Right: Gola Ferguson and Jap, the dog he described as a "one man army."

We concluded in my first book that the bloodlines of Boss and Tige were likely one-half Plott hound, one-fourth Abel hound and one-fourth Blevins dog. The Abel dog was a renowned hunting hound owned by Dr. Joshua Fanning Abel of Waynesville, North Carolina. Plott historian C.E. "Bud" Lyon of Lake City, South Carolina, agreed that this deduction is possible. However, Lyon used insight provided by his friends Gola Ferguson and Von Plott to arrive at another conclusion.

Lyon maintained that Boss and Tige were the result of a union between Gola Ferguson's Plott female, Trim, with a Blevins male called Jake. Ferguson obtained Trim directly from Von Plott. Thus, Lyon's theory is that Boss and Tige were half Plott hound and half Blevins dog. Lyon added that Ferguson's Jap, often fondly referred to by Gola as his "one-man army," carried a triple cross to the Blevins dogs in his pedigree. Jap was a black dog with brindle trim and was the sire of the renowned Plott hound Pistol Packing Mama, the dam of the legendary Plott's Punie.

There are scores of other examples of the strong Blevins influence as well. Yet the question remains: what were the exact origins of these Blevins dogs? Let's begin with what we know for sure about the Blevins clan and their dogs. Then let's try to determine why the facts are so hard to find.

Most breed historians agree that Blaine Blevins was directly responsible for the origination and refinement of the Blevins line. The Blevins family, like the Plott and Cable clans, were of German descent and eventually settled

Pistol Packing Mama, mother of Plott's Punie.

Plott's Punie, classic Plott hound conformation, with black saddleback and Blevins bloodlines.

among the lofty peaks of Yancey County, North Carolina, in the early 1800s. The Blevinses were notable bear hunters there, and even today the Blevins name remains common in the region. Nevertheless, no one knows much about Blaine Blevins and his illustrious dogs.

The late John Banks hunted and bred Plott dogs in eastern North Carolina for more than half a century. Banks was a lifetime member of both the National Plott Hound Association and American Plott Association and played an integral role in getting the Plott dog recognized as the official state dog of North Carolina in 1989.

A native of Yancey County, North Carolina, Banks spent a good deal of his youth in the late 1940s bear hunting in the mountains of his birth. Banks never met Blaine Blevins personally, but he knew of other Blevins family members, such as Zack or "Zacky" Blevins, who had obtained dogs directly from Blaine.

Banks said that the Blevins dogs were various shades of brindle, mostly dark, but some were almost completely black or had black saddlebacks with brindle trim. They were especially vicious animals, fiercely loyal and protective of their masters, while possessing a keen cold nose. Banks believed that it was Blaine Blevins who originated the Blevins line—*after* first obtaining his foundation stock from Montraville Plott in the late 1800s.

The late Dewey Sharp—whom I profiled in my third book, *Legendary Hunters of the Southern Highlands*—concurred with John Banks regarding the origins of the Blevins dogs. Sharp, a native of Graham County, North Carolina, was almost ninety-nine years old when we first met in 2008. He was likely the last man living then who personally met Blaine Blevins and his fabled Blevins family dogs.

Sharp provided rare firsthand insight into Blaine Blevins and his storied hounds. Sharp said that the Blevins family first moved to Graham County from Yancey County shortly after the Civil War. Dewey suspected that the Blevins clan brought dogs with them to Graham County. But Sharp was adamant that Blaine Blevins already had great bear dogs when they first met in 1929, and he was equally as confident in their origins—from Montraville Plott.

Hack Smithdeal of Johnson City, Tennessee, also recalled Blevins and his dogs living in a remote section of Graham County, not far from the Tennessee state line, as did Gola Ferguson, although Ferguson said that Blevins resided in Swain County, not Graham. Ferguson was quoted as saying that the Blevins dogs were "some of the purest Plotts that he had ever seen."

Plott hounds (*far right and far left*) owned by the Samuel Lovin family in Graham County, North Carolina. This is the earliest-known photo of Plott dogs, taken in about 1880. *Courtesy of Marshall McClung.*

Montraville Plott and pup.

Graham County was a hotbed for the Plott breed by the late 1920s. Hunters obtained their Plott hounds from one another, as well as directly from the Plott clan. Certainly, the John Denton and Sam Lovin families are proof of this, as were local lawyers Marshall Bell and Jack Dillard, all of whom obtained their dogs directly from Montraville Plott.

This coincides nicely with what Von Plott discussed in 1973 and 1976 regarding the multitude of renowned mountain bear hunters who rode into Plott Valley on horses or mules in the late 1800s and early 1900s to get Plott pups from his father, Montraville Plott.

This was referred to as the "tow sack network" in my first book, as these celebrated nimrods would enter the Plott farm with an empty tow sack and leave with it filled with purebred Plott pups. Von Plott described it this way:

> *I've seen 'em come by mule and horseback from sections all over these mountains—Robbinsville, Bryson City, Murphy, down in South Carolina and Georgia and over in Tennessee, from all over—and leave with dogs. They'd ride in with an empty tow sack and leave with it full of pups. My daddy would give them to folks with the understanding we could breed back to them if we wanted to. People knew they were special and held up their end of the deal—they didn't just breed them to anything. That way we always had pure bred Plott dogs to fall back on if we needed them.*

In the mid-1960s, Von Plott provided a short list of the folks in the tow sack network to C.E. "Bud" Lyon. The roster included these illustrious southern mountain families: the Denton, Evans, Cruse, Wells, Reece, Hannah, Phillips, Cheek, Monteith, Wiggins, Parker, Lovin, Orr and Rose families, as well as the Blevins and Cable clans.

Lyon concurred with the assessment of Sharp and Banks and added that Gola Ferguson told him that Blaine Blevins obtained Plott hounds directly from Montraville Plott on six to eight different occasions—making the journey repeatedly to Plott Valley in the late 1800s and early 1900s. Ferguson said that these dogs were the foundation stock of the Blevins line. This further verifies that Blevins was adhering to a strict line breeding program. Moreover, it clearly indicates that even with the outside outcrosses that Blevins likely made, the predominant bloodlines of his dogs were purebred Plotts.

But Lyon has additional proof too. Lyon was good friends with Isaiah Kidd of Sinks Grove, West Virginia. Bud said that Kidd remembered receiving a brindle Plott pup from a Blevins family member when he was only eight years old in about 1890. Mr. Kidd was told that the Blevins man had moved to West Virginia from his home in Western North Carolina to find work in the logging industry. Kidd stated that Blevins acquired the pup directly from the Plott family in Waynesville, North Carolina. This is further indication that the Blevins dogs were purebred Plotts, and again, the time frame fits as well.

Additional documentation indicates that the Blevins clan and their dogs maintained a strong presence in West Virginia well beyond the 1890s, through at least to the late 1940s. The Saturday, October 30, 1948 edition of the *Beckley Herald* newspaper tells of renowned local bear hunter Lonnie Blevins and his Plott dogs being joined on a successful bear hunt with friends from Graham County in Western North Carolina and their Plott dogs. This further substantiates the Blevins family connection to Graham County.

The picture was getting clearer, but it still seemed strange as to why information about Blaine Blevins and his dogs is so hard to find and why there are so little records of them today. Dewey Sharp provided a simple answer in 2008. Blevins preferred to keep a low profile to avoid revenuers. Nathaniel "Blaine" Blevins was well known for several things—his musical skills, his fine dogs and, most of all, making outstanding liquor.

Blevins lived "off the grid" in a rugged and remote section of western Graham County near the Tennessee state line, not far from the head of Santeetlah Creek. It provided him sanctuary to not only hunt and raise his renowned hounds but also, more importantly, make moonshine and avoid the law.

When Sharp was asked to clarify Blevins's name (was it Nathaniel or Blaine?), he maintained that his name was Nathaniel Blaine Blevins. Tax and census records indicate that his legal name was Nathaniel Blevins, so that fits too. Dewey had no doubts that Nathaniel and Blaine Blevins were one and the same fellow. He shared a funny story about a holiday shindig held at the Blevins place in 1929. The yarn is included in my third book.

The strong arguments made by breed legends like Gola Ferguson, Von Plott, Bud Lyon, Dewey Sharp, Isaiah Kidd and John Banks that the Blevins dogs were *mostly* purebred Plotts, obtained originally from Montraville Plott, validates their origins. These reputable sources, their extensive knowledge of the subject and the scores of old-time handwritten and UKC-approved pedigrees that we have copies of further solidifies the argument.

However, questions regarding the actual origins of the Blevins hounds remain unanswered. Did the Blevins family, as Sharp suspected, bring dogs with them to Graham County after the Civil War? And if so, what were their bloodlines? Were they mixed-breed mongrels? Or were they a carefully refined strain developed for years by the Blevins family?

It seems more likely that they never brought dogs with them at all and, just as our experts have stated, obtained their dogs instead from the Plott family—or, at the very least, line bred their own dogs religiously to Plott hounds. Based on the information presented here, this makes the most sense to me. However, no one knows for sure and probably never will.

But midwestern Plott breed legend A.F. Stegenga, an esteemed dog breeder from Iona, Michigan, firmly believed that the Blevins dogs were a totally separate strain or bloodline developed and refined entirely by Blaine Blevins with no help whatsoever from the Plott clan. He physically described the Blevins dogs as being mostly black in color, with a strong voice and keen nose.

Furthermore, Stegenga was adamant in his beliefs that the Plott family dogs, in his words, were "headed into obscurity" in the 1920s and fading fast until Gola Ferguson infused the Blevins dog into the Plott line in 1928. The result of that outcross was a dog Stegenga called "second to none."

Moreover, Stegenga maintained that the Plott family later salvaged their line by buying dogs from Ferguson and added that "the greatest work in breeding the Plott line was done *outside* of the Plott family." In fact, Stegenga felt so strongly about this that he was one of a small contingent that argued against naming the first officially registered dogs Plott hounds. Instead, this group argued, the breed should be called Blevins hounds.

Stegenga made bold declarative statements regarding the origins of the Blevins dogs, as well as the decline of the Plott family stock, in a 1947 magazine article entitled "The Plott Hound" that was published in *Bob Becker's Dog Digest.* That same article was later reprinted in the *1959 NPHA Yearbook.*

Gola Ferguson strongly contested this theory. He disagreed with Stegenga and credited the Plott family repeatedly with getting him started in the dog business. So, too, do the other previously noted breed icons.

It should also be noted that the Plott family dogs were stronger than ever between 1900 and 1950. Most of the first dogs registered in 1946 originated from Plott family kennels. UKC records indicate that the Plott clan registered at least fifty Plott hounds between 1946 and 1950. Von Plott bought at least twenty-two of his own hounds on three different trips to Michigan to hunt between 1946 and 1949. There was certainly no shortage of fine Plott family dogs during this era, as their existence and success is well documented. Mr. Stegenga's argument regarding these topics is totally invalid and easily disproven.

This in no way detracts from the Blevins legacy or their importance in breed history. Nor is any disrespect intended toward Mr. Stegenga, who was instrumental in getting the Plott breed recognized by the UKC in 1946. Instead, it simply offers a new perspective on the Blevins legacy and allows the reader to form his or her own opinion on Blevins breed origins.

The story of the Cable clan and their Cable hounds is much easier to trace. It is like the Blevins tale in some ways and entirely different in others, but no less compelling.

THE CABLE CONNECTION

Caspar Cable—born as Kaspar Goebell in his native homeland of Germany in 1755—first arrived in America in 1775 while serving as a Hessian soldier conscripted to fight for the British in the American Revolution. Many historians mistakenly refer to Hessians as individual guns for hire—mercenaries who offered their services to the highest bidder. But they were actually German military units employed to fight for the British, who found it easier to pay the German government for military assistance than to recruit their own citizens.

The name *Hessian* is derived from the German state of Hesse-Kassel, where more than 40 percent of the thirty thousand Hessian soldiers were born. These professional soldiers were fierce, well-disciplined warriors who, although serving the British, fought together in their own units under the German flag and under German command.

Caspar Cable was among the nine hundred Hessian troops captured on Christmas night 1776 at the Battle of Trenton. The Hessians were caught by surprise when General George Washington and his Continental army made their famous crossing of the Delaware River after nearly freezing to death at their Valley Forge encampment.

Apparently, Cable was later part of a prisoner exchange and returned to British service in 1777. Hessian troops fought in almost every major battle in the American Revolution and were highly respected adversaries—so much so that General Washington issued an order offering a large parcel of land, two pigs, a cow and American citizenship to any Hessian soldier willing to defect and join the American army.

Young Caspar Cable couldn't resist this offer and deserted the British at the siege of Charles Town in 1779. It was a gutsy move, as the war was going poorly for the Americans then and it was standard regulation for any Hessian deserters to be beaten severely by their entire company and then executed. Nevertheless, it proved to be the right move, as Cable defected to the American army of General Nathanael Greene and served with Greene for the remainder of the conflict.

After the war ended in 1783, Cable married Elizabeth Baker and settled on the frontier in the Piedmont of North Carolina. He and Elizabeth would eventually have twelve children, including six sons. They lived along the Uwharrie River until 1790, when Caspar moved his family to Wilkes County in the mountains of Western North Carolina. By 1800, he had acquired 150 acres on Dry Run, a tributary of the Watauga River, at Hodges Gap, near the Tennessee border.

It was prime hunting country, abundant with all types of wild game, and very dangerous, as it was technically still Cherokee territory. By all accounts, the Cables were already highly acclaimed hunters well known for their outstanding hunting hounds. Although no one knows for sure the exact origin of these dogs, based on their family history and later photos, it is likely that they were mixed-breed curs.

Three of Caspar Cable's six sons fought in the War of 1812, further honing their hunting and shooting skills. But regarding the Cable dog connection, our focus going forward will be on Samuel Cable, the fifth son of Caspar, who was born in Ashe County, North Carolina, in 1796, along with Sam's son, John Cable Sr., and several of their offspring.

Always searching for better farmland and hunting grounds, newly married Samuel Cable moved to Cades Cove, Tennessee, in 1825. The first of his eight children was born there in 1826. His most famous son, John Baker Cable Sr., was born there in 1828. In 1835, Sam Cable moved his family across the mountain into North Carolina and became one of the earliest white settlers on Hazel Creek in what is now Swain County in the GSMNP.

The Cable clan's new home was a huge tract of land running from lower Hazel Creek and the Little Tennessee River to the top of Welch Ridge. The community and the small tributary running into Hazel Creek became known as Cable Branch. It was here—and throughout the Hazel Creek Watershed—that the Cable family and their Cable hounds would achieve national notoriety. (We will explore this historic area in more detail in chapter 5.)

HAZEL CREEK

Cable Branch and the surrounding region of the Hazel Creek Watershed proved to be an ideal place for the Cable family to further refine their hunting skills and their remarkable line of hunting dogs. It was a pristine wilderness, thick with game, shared by only a few Cherokee neighbors who had avoided removal during the tragic Trail of Tears in the late 1830s.

The Cables—like most mountain families of that era—were blessed with many children, and most of them married and subsequently had large families of their own. Almost all the male Cable siblings were outstanding hunters and dog breeders. But few were more impressive than John Baker Cable Sr., who by the mid-1870s had assumed the role as patriarch of the clan.

John Sr. was ten years old when he moved with his family to Cable Branch in 1835. Young John thrived in the backwoods and liked nothing more than hunting and running the family dogs. He later married a Hazel Creek neighbor, Prudie Marcus, and the couple had at least nine children, five of whom became renowned bear hunters and dog men. They included Sam, William, Joseph, Hezikiah (Kie) and Isaac. But it was a sixth son, John Jr., who became the most famous of them all.

Little John Cable and Coaly.

John Baker Cable Jr., better known as "Little John," was born in 1855. He learned the skills of bear hunting and dog breeding early from the masters—his father and brothers. Little John's brother Joseph was regarded as the best hunter of the brood, and Little John copied his every move. Little John was only five years old in 1860 when he saw Joseph harvest a bruin weighing over 450 pounds. A fierce passion was ignited within Little John to match or exceed the achievements of his storied relatives, and he did exactly that.

Little John added blacksmithing and gun building skills to his vast array of talent as he grew into manhood. He built his own muzzle-loading rifle that

Fonz Cable and Coaly II.

he killed more than one hundred bears with while hunting behind his Cable hounds. He and his wife—the former Nancie Jones—had seven children, including sons William Alfonso ("Fonz"), Daniel and twins Jake and Hezikiah, all of whom carried on the Cable family tradition of bear hunting and bear dogs. Fonz Cable would later bring additional fame to the Cable name as a hunter and dog breeder, and his brother Jake continued the Cable family tradition of service to their country as a soldier in World War I.

By 1900, at the age of forty-five, Little John Cable was widely recognized as one of the best bear hunters in the region, and his dogs were second to none. In a time and place populated with such legendary hunters and Plott dog men as John Denton, Andy Orr, Mark Cathey, Quill Rose, Granville Calhoun, Wilburn Parker, Doc Jones and too many others to list them all, Little John Cable was at or near the top of that illustrious list.

Stories abound pertaining to the amazing talents of the Cable clan and their dogs. Cable hounds were noted for their tenacity and what hunters call "tree power." The term indicates that the dog will tree or bay their prey and stay there until the hunter arrives to kill the bear or coon—no matter how long it takes their master to arrive.

The Cables and their dogs hunted hard and often, six days a week, right up until midnight on Saturday evening. But being dedicated Christians, the Cable clan firmly adhered to the belief of resting on the Sabbath day, reserving it only for worship and fellowship and nothing else.

It was not unusual for them to have a bear (or coon) treed on Saturday night but cease hunting at midnight to observe the Sabbath. Most wrongly assumed that the Cables would leash up their dogs and return home, leaving the bear to escape. But that was not the case. A big family required a lot of food, and a chance for bear meat could not be wasted. The Cables would instead leave their pack of dogs at the bear tree under strict orders to remain there until the clan returned early Monday morning. Without fail, the Cable hounds would still have the bear treed when the hunting party returned to harvest the bruin—more than twenty-four hours later!

Many folks scoffed at this story and sought to disprove it. The next time a similar situation occurred, a local hunter returned to the bear tree on Sunday morning to observe the dogs in action. Sure enough, all six Cable dogs still had the bear treed. But much to his amazement, the man was shocked to find that the dogs were working in shifts as a team to achieve their objective. Three would stay at the tree baying the bear while the other three hounds rested. This rotation continued until the Cables returned on Monday morning.

Another fascinating Cable dog tale involves the logging boom that began on Hazel Creek in the early 1900s. The Cable clan, devoted hunters and farmers, cared nothing for the logging industry, seeing it as detrimental to the independent life they loved. Nevertheless, they were forced to deal with the distraction and work around it.

Little John had a superb female hunting dog during the logging boom that he considered one of his all-time best. She had recently whelped a litter of pups and was locked in a barn stall nursing her pups and recuperating from their birth. John was disappointed that she was unable to hunt but knew that it was in her best interest to stay in the barn and rest. Cable also knew that he would need to tie the dog to further ensure that she did not follow them on the hunting trail.

The gyp sensed that her master had gone hunting and, after a few hours, somehow managed to escape. Little John and his party had a two-hour lead, and the dog inherently knew that she had to find a way to make up lost time. She raced out the barn door headed straight for the nearest rail crossing.

Fonz Cable and Cable hounds. Note the color of these Cable dogs—these are more like Walkers.

Lumber companies, such as Ritter Lumber, had built their own railroad lines deep into the Smokies to haul logs to market in the early 1900s. The narrow-gauge railroads were powered by Shay steam locomotives, which pulled flatbed railcars for hauling logs. Far up the trail, Little John Cable and his party waited as an engine lumbered past them as it climbed slowly toward Eagle Creek.

As the last empty car approached them, Cable was shocked to see his prize gyp sitting proudly on it. The magnificent female jumped from the slow-moving train to join her master on the hunt. This may be a tall tale, but it's a good one if it is, and either way, it further illustrates the reputation for intelligence and tenacity that the Cable hounds enjoyed.

But what were the origins of these incredible Cable dogs? And how were they connected to the Plott breed? It has been a question that has been debated for years, but thanks to the well-documented history of the Cable clan and their close connection to Horace Kephart, the answer appears to be simple.

The Cable clan were renowned hunters on the American frontier since the late 1700s. They were of Germanic origin, and they took their dogs with them as they continually migrated westward, just as the Plott family did. These dogs apparently were a combination of breeds refined by the Cable family over several generations, but predominantly cur. Cable family oral history further confirms this theory, as do photos from the early 1900s. These photos are particularly interesting, as unlike purebred Plotts, the Cable hounds came in a wide variety of colors and sizes and lacked uniformity in appearance.

Even so, like the Blevins connection, the Cable connection is nonetheless speculative—albeit well-documented speculation. However, unlike the Blevins connection, we have documented proof straight from the proverbial horse's mouth regarding the pedigree of the Cable hounds. No less an authority than Little John Cable himself explained it in detail to acclaimed writer Horace Kephart in Kephart's 1913 book, *Our Southern Highlanders*.

KEPHART'S BEAR HUNT

Writer Horace Kephart had written outdoor-themed articles in national magazines since at least 1895 and was once a highly regarded librarian in St. Louis, Missouri. Kephart left his family and moved to the Great Smoky Mountains region in 1904, looking for solace, peace and healing in what he called "the back of beyond."

He found what he was looking for and lived on Hazel Creek for almost three years between 1904 and 1907. Kephart resided in the Smokies—in or around Bryson City, North Carolina—until his death in 1931. It was here that he became world famous.

Although he did not live to see it, Kephart played an integral role in the formation of the Great Smoky Mountains National Park, and in addition to his numerous magazine articles, Kephart wrote two classic books and several lesser-known titles. All remain in print today, but Kephart is best known for *Camping and Woodcraft* (1906) and *Our Southern Highlanders* (1913). Both were immediate bestsellers.

Many critics felt that Kephart's work—most notably *Our Southern Highlanders*—unfairly stereotyped all mountaineers as uncouth, backward, uneducated hillbillies. Yet others argue that Kephart was extremely well liked and respected among locals and that his portrayals were not intended to be indicative of the entire region but were only intended as thumbnail sketches of selected individuals—all of whom he held in high regard.

We'll leave it to more qualified scholars to sort that argument out. I can see both sides, as the title itself would seem to be indicative of the entire region and its inhabitants. Yet the dialect, the dialogue, the character profiles and many of the stories—especially that of the 1912 bear hunt—are spot-on correct. Plus, it could be argued that Kephart's funeral in 1931 remains one of the largest ever held in the county and that this alone indicates the high esteem in which he was held by locals.

Moreover, Kephart was allowed to hunt with such esteemed bear hunters as Little John Cable, Quill Rose, Granville Calhoun and others, further validating that he was highly respected as a friend and woodsman. These men did not suffer fools lightly and took their sport and their dogs seriously.

Kephart was not paying them as guides, nor was he a flunky whom they simply tolerated. He clearly was considered a respected peer. But regardless of what they thought of him personally, Kephart's experiences on the 1912 hunt provide us with a treasure-trove of information regarding old-time mountain bear hunting, hunters, bear dogs and, more specifically, the origins of the Cable hound.

The writer was enamored of both the hunters and their dogs, admiring the stamina, marksmanship, woodcraft and discipline of these nimrods, saying that they could make superb soldiers under "the leadership of a backwoods Napoleon like Daniel Morgan." Whether Kephart was aware of it or not, the ancestors of most of these men—including the Cables—had indeed fought bravely in every American war since the Revolution.

Kephart enjoyed the camp camaraderie, tall tales and superstitions, as he shares numerous yarns told by Doc Jones, Bill Hyde and Little John Cable, along with technical insight on how the hunt was conducted, mountain superstitions and how the bear meat was separated fairly among the hunting party.

But most of all, Kephart was intrigued with the Cable dogs: "The dogs were powerful beasts, dangerous to man and to the brutes they were trained

A 1919 photo of legendary Hall hunting cabin on Thunderhead Mountain, site of bear hunt in Kephart's *Our Southern Highlanders*. *Courtesy of GSMNP Archives.*

to fight, although Little John was clearly their master. They are true bear dogs who knew no such word as quit."

The hunters were camped in the Hall Cabin high on the Tennessee/North Carolina border—not to be confused with the Crate Hall Cabin on Hazel Creek. Kephart indicated that there were at least four bear dogs huddled among them in the building seeking warmth as they rode out a winter storm. They included Cable's youngest dog, Coaly, on his first bear hunt, and another veteran Cable hound known as Dred. Apparently, the third dog, a female called Towse, was also of Cable lineage, while the fourth canine was a Plott hound named Rock, owned by Doc Jones.

Coaly was injured on his first hunt, but Cable is not the least bit concerned as to whether the dog was still game, as he added, "If he has his daddy and mammy's grit, we'll find out tomorrow." This further indicates the proven strategy of understanding your bloodlines and breeding the best to the best. Cable had purposely bred a proven superior bitch to a superb, proven stud and was confident that good bloodlines would prevail—and they did.

Coaly earned his spurs the next two days, baying two bears despite his injuries. Kephart noted, "Three days ago Coaly was an inconsequential pup, but soon he looked into my eyes with the calm dignity that no fool or braggart can assume. He had been knighted. He licked his wounds and was proud of them—the scars of battle, sir. You may have your swagger ribbons and prize collars in a New York dog show—but this is for me."

The scribe concluded his story with the tale of Coaly's tragic demise two years later. Kephart wrote that he had traded or sold a new 30.30 rifle to Granville Calhoun, who was a close friend and hunting partner to both Kephart and the Cable family. Another mutual friend, Quill Rose, is quoted as saying that he hated these modern rifles, disdainfully calling them "power guns" due to the likelihood of them shooting through a bear and killing a dog or another hunter. Kephart reported that Calhoun did exactly that in 1914—shooting a bear with his new rifle and killing both the bear and Coaly in the process.

Kephart was rightfully impressed with these dogs. He had also done his homework regarding what were already considered the best bear dogs in the world, the Plott hound. Plott family handwritten pedigrees dating back to the early 1900s list Cable dogs several times in their bloodlines, although their lineage was predominantly dogs line bred by the Plott family and their friends Wilburn Parker and John Denton.

Clearly there was a connection here. But was it a case of a totally separate outcross? Or was it like the Blevins theory, basically a purebred Plott with a little something extra added but still essentially a purebred Plott? Horace Kephart answered these questions for us as he interviewed Little John Cable: "John, are these dogs of yours Plott hounds? Have they got the Plott strain? I have been told that purebred Plott hounds are the best bear dogs in the country."

Little John snorted this reply: "Tain't so—Plott curs are the best, that is a half Plott hound, half cur cross, although what we call a cur in this case really comes from a big foreign dog that I don't rightly know the breed of."

Was Cable saying that he crossed a purebred Plott with the family Cable curs to get the perfect bear dog? Or is he saying that the perfect combination is one-fourth Plott, one-fourth cur and one-half Cable dog? It's hard to say, but I think he answered the question as Kephart asked him to elaborate.

Cable added, "You can talk as you please about a streak of cur spoiling a dog, but it ain't so—not for bear fighting in these mountains, where you can't follow on horseback, but have to do your own running."

"Why is that?" Kephart asked. Cable answered:

> *It's like this. A plumb cur can't follow a cold track—he just runs by sight and he won't hang—he quits. No hound will really fight a bear either. It takes a severe dog to do that. Hounds has the best noses, and they'll run a*

> *bear all day, all night, and the next day too, but they won't tree. They are afraid to close in. Now, look at them dogs of mine—a cur ain't got no dew claws—them dogs has. My dogs can follow ANY trail, just like a hound, but then they will run right in on that varmint, snappin', chawin.' And worrying him until he gets so mad that you can hear the bears tushes a popping half a mile away. Finally, the bear gets so tired he runs up a tree to rest—then we finish him.*

Based on the Cable clan's storied hunting history on the American frontier and the fact that they always had their own dogs, combined with the testimony of no less an authority than Little John Cable and the photos of dogs owned by Fonz Cable, it seems to me that the origins of the Cable dogs are clear, as are their connections to the Plott hound.

The Cables started with their own dogs—a big cur of foreign origins. Not satisfied with their nose, they then bred them to a Plott hound or another breed of scent hound, or possibly both, to further refine the breed. They continued to do this in different variations until they achieved their desired objective.

The result was the dog we know as the Cable hound, a canine distinctly different from, yet related to, a Plott hound. The Plott family—particularly Montraville Plott and his sons John and Von Plott—were impressed enough to add them to their own bloodlines, and the Cables eagerly added Plott hounds to their family lineage as well. This is yet another example of a likely outside outcross and why many people wanted to see the Cable dogs registered as a separate breed with the UKC in 1946.

The debate on the specific origins of the Blevins dogs and the Cable hounds and their infusion into the Plott line continues today more than a century after the events first occurred. The argument likely will never be conclusively resolved to the satisfaction of all parties involved.

But one thing is for certain: the remarkable story of the Plott breed and the Appalachian legends that helped perpetuate it is a rich and storied one with many intricate layers. The Blevins dog, the Blevins family and the Cable hound and Cable clan *did* indeed play integral roles in Plott breed history. Regardless of how they originated, how many times it was outcrossed or how their lineage was introduced into the Plott hound line, the Plott breed is better for it.

CHAPTER 4

WILBURN PARKER

"King of the Balsam Bear Hunters"

The Great Balsams and Plott Balsams are two of the highest mountain ranges in the southern Appalachian Mountains. Located in Haywood and Jackson Counties in Western North Carolina, the range contains at least nine peaks exceeding the height of six thousand feet. The Balsams cover about 822 square miles of rugged terrain, while giving rise to three important regional waterways: the Pigeon, French Broad and Tuckasegee Rivers.

The mountains are named for the Fraser fir and red spruce trees that densely populate their higher elevations and for the Plott family—some of the earliest white settlers in the area, renowned for both their hunting skills and their Plott bear hounds. For centuries, the Balsam Range has been prime habitat for black bears and all sorts of wildlife, and it is where the Plott hound first gained regional recognition. But long before the arrival of the white man, the mountains were primary hunting grounds for the Cherokee tribe who made their homes here and in nearby valley villages.

One of the best Cherokee bear hunters was the iconic Cherokee chief Yonaguska. He lived near Soco Gap and was one of the many early bear hunting legends of the Balsam Mountains. Henry Plott, along with his descendants Amos, Enos, Robert Henry, Montraville, Herbert, Von, John, Sam, Cecil and Little George Plott, were all notable regional bear hurting icons as well. So, too, were Mark Reece, Fed Messer, numerous members of the Rich clan and Israel "Wid" Medford—the self-proclaimed "master bear hunter of the Balsams." All of them were profiled in my previous books.

However, it was arguably Wilburn Parker who is most deserving of the title bestowed on him by the writer John Parris as "King of the old-time Balsam bear hunters." Parker, like John Denton, is also a prime example of the "tow sack network" described in the last chapter. He was a fierce proponent of line breeding in his hunting dog program, as he sought to consistently perpetuate the Plott family bloodlines. Parker descendants maintain that Wilburn seldom, if ever, deviated with any outside outcrosses—always staying true to the original Plott breeding formula. Early handwritten Plott family pedigrees dating to about 1900 further verify this fact, as Parker's dogs are prominently mentioned there, particularly his famous Hardwood dog.

It seems fitting that the story of the king of the Balsam bear hunters begins in the kingdom in which he would eventually reign—at the base of the Plott Balsam Range in the Caney Fork Township of Jackson County, North Carolina.

EARLY LIFE

Joseph Wilburn Parker's early life is shrouded in mystery. Even his date of birth has been the source of debate. Some sources, like writer John Parris, suggest that Parker was born on September 9, perhaps as early as 1860, while others indicate that he was born on that same September date but as late as 1876. Parker's 1917 draft registration papers indicate that he was born in 1873.

Official county records aren't much help, as they only offer an approximate birthdate of "around 1875." Federal census records from 1910 and 1930 offer differing birth dates as well. The 1910 census indicates 1875 as Parker's year of birth, while the 1930 census lists that he was born in 1874. Parker's tombstone also indicates he was born in 1874. That date is probably closer to the truth, so we will go with that.

Parker's specific bloodlines aren't clear either. His parents are officially listed as John Mills Parker and Martha Parker, both highly respected residents of the Caney Fork community near Cullowhee, North Carolina. However, there are also rumors that Parker was born out of wedlock to a local woman and adopted by the Parker family as an infant. Parker descendant Eddie Parker said that this isn't true. It doesn't matter much either way, as Wilburn Parker was a devoted son to John and Martha Parker, whom he considered his true parents.

Details of Parker's youth and formative years are sketchy as well. The 1910 federal census indicates that Parker was capable of reading and writing.

However, the 1930 census says that he never attended school and was basically illiterate. Whatever Wilburn may or may not have lacked in formal education, he was undoubtedly highly intelligent. It is equally clear that like most youngsters in this time and place, Parker learned the skills of woodcraft and hunting early on. Hunting was more than just sport to Wilburn, his kinfolk and neighbors—it was a matter of survival. Almost everyone was good at it, as they had to be, but young Wilburn Parker was exceptional.

Parker grew into manhood described as being of medium height but broad shouldered and powerfully built, with the strength and stamina of a packhorse. Parker had coal-black hair, and by his twenty-first birthday, he had grown an impressive handlebar moustache that he wore the remainder of his life.

Although he hunted deer, turkey and all sorts of small game from the time he could walk, Parker never bear hunted until his twenty-first birthday in 1895 (assuming that the 1874 birthdate is correct). In those days, many hunters still used single-shot muzzle-loading rifles, and powder and shot were at a premium. Old-time bear hunters subscribed strongly to the one shot/one kill theory, as every shot was critical, and only the very best of hunters could shoot a dangerous bear.

Even though he was already a crack shot and had hunted successfully with legendary bear hunters like Jim Cook and Jerry Wood for years, Wilburn was relegated to the role of chief dog handler until he turned twenty-one. Parker recalled the details of killing his first bear to John Parris in articles first written by Parris in 1933 and 1934:

> *I'll never forget it. It was my 21st birthday, September 9, when I brought down old number one! Jim Cook and Jerry Wood were two old-time bear hunters who knew how to hunt bear. I was fortunate that they took me under their wing. They learned me early how to shoot straight and fast. I was just a strapping of a boy and I could get around good in the woods. I knew a lot about dogs and how to hunt them too. But up until then they'd never even allow me to carry my own gun. I only handled the dogs and helped carry the dead bear out. That was it.*

Parker paused to switch his quid of chewing tobacco to his left jaw before continuing his story to Parris:

> *I finally bucked up enough nerve to Uncle Jerry and told him I was going to bring my gun. Jerry said, no, you ain't, you're going to take care of the*

> *dogs like always—that's what we need you for. Uncle Jim Cook felt sorry for me, and we convinced Jerry to let me take my gun.*

Pausing to spit, Wilburn finished his tale:

> *We struck a bear track and turned the dogs loose. The first thing you know, the bear breaks the brush and busted into the open. Right then and there I let that old bruin have it good and plenty. I shot him with an old muzzle loading hog rifle, loaded with black powder and a patched bullet-ball. I floored him with a prime shot—right in the critter's heart!*

It wasn't long after that when two major changes took place in Parker's life. The first involved upgrading his pack of bear hounds—we'll discuss that in detail shortly. Parker's second change involved finding a wife. He addressed that when he married the love of his life, a distant cousin, Ida Alice Parker, in 1895. The couple were blessed with eight children, all of whom became stellar hunters and crack shots. Wilburn proudly described them to John Parris in 1935:

> *All my family is good shots, from Maw, Ida, right on down to every one of the kids. We have eight children—five boys and three girls. And all of them, even Maw and the girls, like to bear hunt with their Pa, and all of them can shoot the wings off a gnat.*

After marrying his soul mate, Wilburn started his own family. They lived first in Caney Fork in Jackson County, North Carolina. Sometime around 1910, the couple bought a farm in Haywood County, North Carolina, along the west fork of Pigeon River near the Sunburst Community. Parker further supplemented his income by working as a warden for the Sherwood Forest Lumber Company and as a hunting guide for various regional hunting clubs—including several clubs described in chapter 5—while also serving as a deputy sheriff and fire warden in Haywood County.

KING OF THE BALSAMS

By 1936, Parker was widely recognized as one of the best bear hunters in a region known for great ones. Writers from across the country flocked to

Western North Carolina to record the exploits of Wilburn Parker and his Plott hounds. J.B. Hicklin of the *New York Times* wrote on November 8, 1936, that "Wilburn Parker, the Dean of the North Carolina bear hunters, stalks bear in the wild Balsam mountains with the ease of a city man strolling down a sidewalk to his downtown office."

John Parris wrote multiple articles about Parker between 1933 and 1980 and first crowned him the "King of the old-time Balsam bear hunters" in a 1933 column in the *Asheville Citizen Times*. In later years, Parris wrote that Parker harvested more than one hundred bruins in his illustrious hunting career and was in on the killing of that many or more. Many of the bears were killed with an ancient twelve-gauge shotgun that Parris noted was battle scarred with tooth and claw marks from bears fought at close range. Parris remembered first meeting Parker when Wilburn was about sixty years old and being impressed with his vitality and woods wisdom.

Even as an older man with hair and mustache snowy white, Parris wrote that seeing Parker was like a "picture, never to be forgotten." Parris, a master storyteller who appreciated a good story, considered Parker a raconteur second to none and greatly admired his wry sense of humor. Wilburn shared this story with Parris in 1934:

> *I expect to skin well over a hundred bears before I pass across the great divide, and I got a long time to live yet. I am a long way from being done. I may live to be 100 years old, and if I do, I'm sure going to make it hard and hot for the bears in this country. And let me tell you something else—my life goes on despite the New Deals and the such. The Great Depression has meant nothing to me. I have lived royally for years and I am still doing so.*

Writer J.B. Hinklin echoed John Parris's sentiments and offered this humorous anecdote pertaining to Parker's preferred recipe for bear meat:

> *Get you a prime piece of bear meat, a ham, a roast or back strap, then you put it in a kettle, and fill it with water and build you a good hot fire under it. Once you get that water to good boil, throw in some salt, pepper and spices, then last, but not least, pitch in about six or seven good sized river rocks. Let it all cook good and slow for about six hours. Then throw out the dang bear meat and eat the river rocks!*

Unlike their esteemed father, four of Parker's sons loved bear meat. And the boys were equally renowned bear hunters as well. John Parris

Wilburn Parker and his wife, Ida, with son, Frank. *Courtesy of Eddie Parker.*

wrote of Wilburn's exciting hunt with one of his sons, Herbert, in the early 1930s. The hunt took place on Green Mountain in Haywood County, North Carolina, where Herbert Parker saved the life of one of his father's best dogs:

> *We was running a big bear, well over 700 pounds, when it turned on my best dog, we called him Hardwood. That big rascal was about to squeeze old Hardwood to death, until my boy, Herbert, saved his life. Herbert loved that dog, and he just waded in there and grabbed that big old bear by the head with one hand, and then with the other hand, he jammed his rifle against its head and fired point blank. Killed that bear dead, blew his brains out—and saved Hardwood's life!*

Parris also submitted a report in the *Asheville Citizen Times* regarding a 1933 bear hunt with Wilburn and three of his sons—Ralph, Lester and Herbert, all of whom were at least twenty-six years old by that time. The hunt took place on Beech Ridge in the Bear Wallow section of the Balsam Mountains in Jackson County. Parris stated that the hunting party consisted of fifteen local hunters and sixteen bear hounds—most of the dogs were owned by Parker and his sons or another local Plott breed hunting legend, Reginald Enloe of Dillsboro, North Carolina. Parris added that the Parker hunting party had slow tracked the bear for a few miles from a farm where it had pillaged several cows, sheep and hogs.

Once a hot trail was struck, the Parker party turned their dogs loose, and the race began. The hunters packed dogs to the track for more than thirty minutes, going well over a mile before finally baying the beast in a thicket where the massive bruin made its last stand. Seven total shots were fired by Herbert, Ralph and Lester Parker, with Lester getting credit for the kill. The rogue boar bear was estimated to have been about six years old and weighed more than five hundred pounds.

Wilburn Parker's hunting expertise and loyalty to the Plott breed make him worthy of mention in any legitimate breed history. But it was his Hardwood Plott line, along with his twenty-five-year search for the giant rogue bear known as Honest John, that truly earned Parker his title as king of the Balsam bear hunters. Let's take a closer look at both those topics.

HARDWOOD ORIGINS AND LINEAGE

Through it all, Parker continually sought to refine his pack of bear hounds. To hunt even more effectively, Wilburn knew from the start that he would need the best dogs around, and he knew where to get them. Parker had first learned of the Plott hound through his mentors, Jim Cook and Jerry Wood, and he was determined to acquire dogs of his own. Parker's bear dog pack refinement plan began in the late 1890s. He first traveled across Balsam Gap by horseback and ventured into Plott Valley, where he acquired at least two purebred Plott pups from Montraville Plott.

Von Plott, with famous Plott dogs including Balsam, Happy and Link.

Parker later befriended Mont Plott's youngest son, Von, and oldest son, John, and obtained dogs from them on a regular basis for at least thirty years. By the time Wilburn had moved his family to Haywood County in 1910, he and his dogs were held in high regard throughout the region. When asked by John Parris in 1933 to describe the origins of his dogs, as well as what made them special, Parker answered this way:

> *I always keep at least nine pure bred Plott dogs in my pack. They were bred by old man Plott, Montraville Plott, who lived over in Plott Valley—he's dead now. I got started with him and I have never seen better or tougher dogs than his. They won't quit, no matter what. I have run Plott dogs after a bear from Jackson County all the way to Sam's Knob in Haywood County—that's at least fifteen miles. Plott hounds are real bear dogs, you can't beat them!*

Parker's first male pup would become known as Hardwood, and the female, from another separate litter, was later bred with Hardwood. These dogs became the foundation stock of Parker's renowned Hardwood Plott hound line. These canines—and their descendants—soon became legendary in the Balsams, further solidifying their connection as being among the best and purest of purebred Plott hounds.

The pup known as Hardwood turned out to be the best Plott bear hound that Wilburn Parker ever owned, followed closely by Hardwood's son Little Hardwood. Both Hardwood and Little Hardwood were also proven sires, repeatedly fathering litters of outstanding pups over the next several years, and those pups, in turn, produced future generations of outstanding hounds.

A quick review of some early handwritten pedigrees generated by the Plott family, along with the earliest UKC registration papers dating back to 1946, 1947 and 1948, further validate this fact. John Plott's Trixie was whelped in 1948 and descended from many famous Plott hounds such as Hack Smithdeal's Blue Joe and Smithdeal's Polly, as well as four of John Denton's dogs and numerous Plott family canines. Along with these illustrious hounds, Hardwood was listed in the back of Trixie four times, and Little Hardwood was included once.

A June 1940 five-generation handwritten Plott family pedigree for Plott's Trim included Plott's Scott, Gola Ferguson's Lady and Boss and Little George Plott's famous Buckskin, along with Wilburn Parker's Hardwood. Five notable Plott dogs on the 1935 Branch Rickey Hazel Creek hunt—Plott's Scott, Dan, Bute, Buckskin and Bess—all had Hardwood bloodlines in their lineage, as did Gola Ferguson's Boss and Tige.

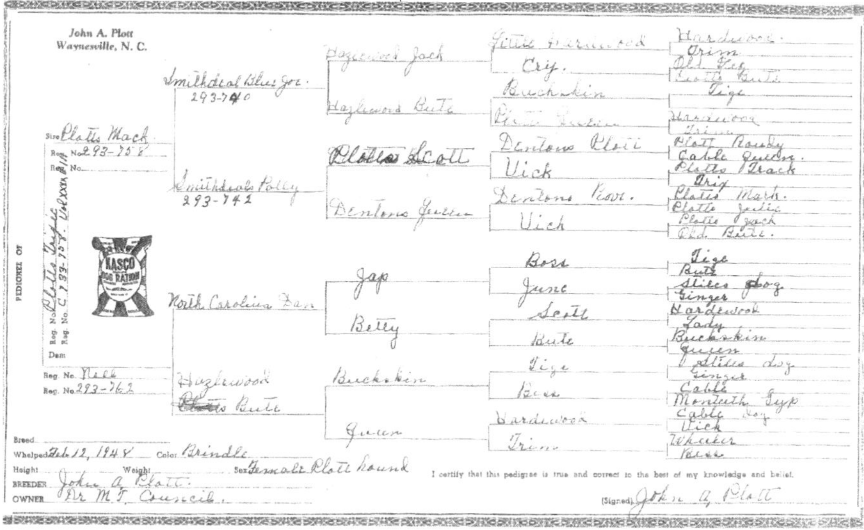

John A. Plott
Waynesville, N. C.

PEDIGREE OF Plotts Trixie

Reg. No. C 293-757. Vol XXXX

Sire Platts Mack
Reg. No. 293-758
Reg. No.

Dam Nell
Reg. No. 293-762

Smithdeal Blue Joe. 293-740
Smithdeals Polly 293-742
North Carolina Dan
Hazlewood Bute

Hazlewood Jack
Hazlewood Bute
Plotts Scott
Dentons Queen
Jap
Betty
Buckskin
Queen

Cry.
Buckskin
Dentons Plott
Vick
Dentons Rover.
Vick
Boss
June
Scott
Bute
Tige
Bess
Hardwood
Trim

Hardwood.
Trim
Old Peg
Tige
Platt Rowdy
Cable Queen.
Platts Track
Trix
Platts Mark.
Platts Julie
Platts Jack
Old Bute.
Tige
Bute
Stiles dog.
Ginger
Hardewood
Lady
Buckskin
Queen
Stiles dog.
Ginger
Cable
Monteith Gyp
Cable dog
Vick
Wheeler
Bess

Breed
Whelped Feb. 12, 1948 Color Brindle
Height Weight Sex Female Plott hound
BREEDER John A. Plott.
OWNER Dr M. T. Council.

I certify that this pedigree is true and correct to the best of my knowledge and belief.

(Signed) John A. Plott

A 1947 handwritten pedigree by John Plott.

Plott's Scott and Dan, two of the earliest Plotts registered by the UKC, and both were on the 1935 Rickey hunt.

Multiple members of the first one hundred Plott dogs registered with the UKC in 1946 also have Hardwood and/or Little Hardwood in their lineage—most notably Plott's Scott, Dan, Plott's Trim and Plott's Belle, along with several more of Gola Ferguson's iconic dogs.

Parker's Hardwood line—along with the previously mentioned Cable, Denton and Blevins dogs—were all integral components of Plott breed history in the early twentieth century, and none were more highly coveted or more closely bred than Parker's renowned hounds. Simply put, the Hardwood line *was* Plott history, and it's easy to see why when you examine these pedigrees. But better yet, listen as Parker explained the virtues of his Hardwood dog and subsequent Hardwood Plott hounds:

> *Hardwood and Little Hardwood were my best early Plott dogs. I was once offered 300 dollars for the original Hardwood. Folks all over knew about old Hardwood. Folks all around here, and in Tennessee, and even up in Virginia and Kentucky had heard of him. He once fought a bear for 24 straight hours. We had to crawl through laurel thickets—it was something awful! Old Hardwood hung on until I got there, he had that bear cornered against a rock cliff in the thicket. I let him have it right between the eyes.*

Parker stopped for a moment as he remembered Hardwood to John Parris, before adding a sad eulogy to his beloved hound: "Someone killed old Hardwood—poisoned him. I was as mad as brimstone and I would have killed the fellow who done it if I could have found out who he was. It was probably a good thing for him and me that I didn't."

As for his later day dogs, Parker told Parris that his best one was a buckskin Plott dog known as Red Bone. He then recounted this story about him and the many attributes of the Plott breed:

> *Red Bone was hurt bad upstream on the Pigeon River. He got his innards ripped out by a mean bear, part of them was laying right there on the ground. I stuffed his guts back in and sewed him up with a Woodchuck leather shoe lace. I thought he was done for. But he recovered about a year later. He still wanted to hunt even when he was hurt. The only way to keep a good Plott dog sewed up and safe is to keep him home. There ain't no quit in them. Bears are smart animals, they think quick—but a good Plott dog is smarter and quicker. They* have *to be to survive.*

Von Plott with a pack of his top Plott hounds, accompanied by his favorite Airedale.

Like his friend Von Plott, Wilburn Parker greatly admired Airedales for their fierce tenacity and always included one or two of them in his usual nine-dog Plott pack. His favorite Airedale was a dog known as Rich. Rich was so tenacious and ferocious that despite being seriously injured, he once latched onto the rear leg of an angry bruin and held on tight as the bear climbed twenty-five feet up a tree. The fierce Airedale held on until being hurled to the ground by the beast just before the bear took his last breath.

Rich survived and was retired to live happily on Parker's front porch the remainder of his life. But Rich was the only one of his kind to survive, as the Airedales were just too ferocious for their own good, usually getting killed or seriously injured after only a few hunts. Parker admired them nevertheless and noted that the Airedales could hunt most any type of game well and could capably track humans too.

The retirement of Rich is yet another example of how well Wilburn Parker treated his dogs, especially his Plott hounds. Parker, like most great hunters, had a special bond with his dogs and treated them like family. He expressed his disgust to John Parris in 1934 regarding how some hunters killed their dogs when they were too old to actively hunt:

> *I wouldn't kill a dog of mine for 1,000 dollars.* [Parker jokingly added,] *I'd just as soon kill my wife or other family member as one of my dogs. No sir, I don't kill my dogs. When they get too old or crippled to hunt, I just let them stay around the house until they die of old age. I feed them as well—if not better—than my dogs still hunting. I owe that to them. They have done their best for me and I am* not *going to kill them or give them away to show my gratitude.*

As Parker's fame as a hunter grew, so, too, did the notoriety of his Hardwood Plott hound line. Other great Parker Plott hounds included Winner, Gun Powder, Wade, Maude, Queen and Snowball, among many others too numerous to mention.

Wilburn Parker had achieved his objective of refining his bear dog pack at precisely the right time. Parker would need every one of his great dogs, and more, as he launched his quest for the outlaw bear, Honest John, around 1912.

Honest John

Southern Appalachian history is filled with stories of notable rogue bears, almost all of them with colorful names, such as Slewfoot, Big Jim, Kettlefoot and Reelfoot, just to name a few. The bruins usually earned their nicknames due to their unusual tracks and massive size, as well as their propensity for destroying domestic livestock such as cattle, sheep and pigs. Almost all of them came to a bad end, killed by bear hunters in usually well-documented circumstances.

The bear known as Honest John was similar in that he had a distinctive paw print and was indeed huge—reportedly well over seven hundred pounds. However, two things set Honest John apart from all others. One was his preference for pork. Honest John would eat or kill nothing else, and he would never kill more than he could eat at any one time. Not being a greedy bruin earned him his moniker.

The second thing that made Honest John unique was that he terrorized the Balsam Range and surrounding region for better than a quarter of a century without getting killed. The National Wildlife Federation states that the average lifespan of a black bear is short—usually about ten to twelve years. However, there have been exceptions where bears have lived thirty

A 1940 photo of a 550-pound bear killed by Rufus Sutton and Frank Rich that some believed was the legendary Honest John. *Courtesy of Steven and Linda Rich.*

years or more. Honest John was one them. It is generally believed that the renegade bruin lived at least thirty-five years, maybe longer.

Honest John was reportedly a young adult bear in 1912—probably not much more than a yearling—when his reign of terror began. The massive beast's campaign against domestic hogs continued for almost three decades.

There was one report that John was later killed by James Rich and Rufus Sutton in 1935. Sutton and Rich harvested a 550-pound bear at the head of Indian Creek, near Soco Gap, North Carolina, in November that same year. Another 1940 report suggested that Frank Rich and Rufus Sutton killed Honest John that year. However, most experts—including, most notably, Wilburn Parker—disputed that the bears killed were Honest John. And if anyone would know, it was Parker, as he had trapped, hunted and tracked the giant bear for years.

Like the revenge-obsessed whaler Captain Ahab in Herman Melville's classic novel *Moby Dick*, Wilburn Parker was determined to kill Honest John at all costs. But unlike Captain Ahab—who detested Moby Dick—Parker truly respected and admired Honest John. Chasing the big bear made life more interesting and gave him something to look forward to. Over the years,

Parker and Honest John became synonymous with each other. One's name was seldom uttered without someone mentioning the other. Wilburn even had his own theory as to why Honest John killed only hogs:

> *I have heard tell that Honest John favors hog meat because of what some razorbacks done to his ma and sisters and brothers. It happened when he was a little fellow. It was just after winter when the mama bear woke up and a pile of them razorbacks got after her. Well, they killed her and all the rest of the litter of cubs except the little one that we now call Honest John. He never forgot that! And he ain't got no use for hogs exceptin' as meat to fill his belly. He is a choosey old cuss. He HAS to have his hog meat, but he'll kill only one—and it's always the best one in the lot.*

Parker's first run-in with Honest John occurred in 1912 on Piney Ridge, high in the Plott Balsams in Jackson County, North Carolina. Although he was yet to earn his famous nickname, Honest John had just begun to raid local farms when he was briefly captured by Parker. Wilburn had set a large steel trap on a local farm and secured it firmly, but it was no match for Honest John. The giant bruin slammed the trap repeatedly against a rock, severing a toe off his left front paw in the process. Honest John finally made his escape, and Parker later agreed that he was glad of it. Such a worthy adversary deserved a more fitting end. Thus began the obsession that would plague Parker for years as he stalked Honest John throughout the Balsam Range.

Not only was Honest John's track now distinctive—with the missing left front toe—but it was huge as well. Parker stated that a large man's hat would not fill one of Honest John's tracks. "He's a big brute, he has the biggest track of any bear in the country. His paws are eleven inches long and seven inches wide. He pushes them into the ground like a big horse—he weighs at least 700 pounds." For decades to come, these distinctive tracks would appear regularly on farms within a forty-mile radius of his den deep in the Balsams, as Honest John earned his name by killing only one pig in each sty.

When he wasn't working or guiding hunts, Parker spent almost every waking moment studying Honest John and trying to figure ways to catch him. In doing so, he learned more about the rogue bear than any man alive. Wilburn spoke of Honest John with a respect bordering on reverence and awe to John Parris in 1934:

Little George Plott (*left*), with Cody Plott, on the trail of Honest John.

> *Honest John is the beatinest bear I have ever heard tell of for making himself scarce. He seems almost human, the way he can sense danger. And the way he can make an escape makes a man wonder if he ain't a ghost! But you know he ain't when you find your best hog killed off, and Honest John's tracks there for all to see.*

Between 1911 and 1940, Wilburn Parker and his Plott dogs continued to rack up record numbers of bear kills. By 1940, they had been directly or indirectly involved in the killing of more than two hundred bruins. Yet despite numerous near misses, Honest John continually eluded the grasp of the master nimrod.

During that same period, Honest John was recording some impressive totals of his own. The rogue bear supposedly killed at least 175 hogs—always one at a time and always the best pig in the lot. Numerous other notable Balsam bear hunters such as Von Plott, Little George Plott, Taylor and Kay Wilson, Cody Plott, Hub Plott, James Rich, Reg Enloe and Rufus Sutton, among others, were also accumulating record-setting bear totals of their own. Yet they also tried and failed to kill the mighty beast.

Signs of Honest John were common up until 1939. But the giant bear had disappeared entirely by the early 1940s. By 1940, Wilburn Parker was at least sixty-six years old, and although he remained a physical force to be reckoned with, the years had taken their toll on the snowy-haired mountain legend. He was frustrated that he was physically no longer able to do the extraordinary things he had done as a younger man. But he found it even more aggravating that he had never killed Honest John, and now his lifelong adversary was nowhere to be found, likely dead and gone for good. It was like losing a friend to the old mountaineer.

Most experts feel that the old rogue bear had simply died of old age. And they were probably right. After all, despite being pursued nonstop for decades by some of the world's best bear hunters and their dogs, Honest John's lifespan had far exceeded that of the typical bruin. Parker agreed with this assessment, yet it felt as if a part of him had died as well.

DEATH OF A LEGEND

With World War II and old age looming on the horizon, and his hunting grounds rapidly disappearing, Wilburn Parker—like a lot of folks in the southern Appalachians—headed to the Pacific Northwest for a fresh start. In 1942, at the age of sixty-eight, the king of the Balsam bear hunters packed up his family and moved to Washington State.

Little is known of his life there. We know that he already had relatives living in the Skagit Valley and that Hamilton, Washington—where Wilburn later made his home—was a booming logging town. But apparently, despite the almost unlimited opportunities for logging jobs and bear hunting, Parker had difficulty adjusting to life on the West Coast. Part of the problem was likely just being homesick, but a bigger issue was Parker's failing health and his frustration in dealing with old age. He simply wasn't the man he used to be; he could not work and hunt like he used to, and that was difficult for anyone to accept—but even more so for a living legend.

Tragically, on September 19, 1947, Wilburn Parker, the king of the Balsam bear hunters, walked out to the toolshed behind his home in Hamilton, Washington, and took his own life. He was seventy-three years old. Parker was buried in the Hamilton Cemetery. His loyal wife, Ida, was buried next to him when she passed away in 1954.

When word of Parker's death reached his beloved Balsam homeland, his friends, family and fellow hunters were understandably distraught. Yet master bear hunter Ed Bumgarner provided a fitting eulogy to both Parker and his counterpart, Honest John, to writer John Parris in 1955: "Honest John just got so old that he had to lay down and die. It seems right that he did, because Wilburn Parker had to lay aside his rifle due to old age too. They are both gone now. But we will never forget them and their spirits will live forever in these mountains."

Indeed. There will never be another outlaw bear like Honest John or another hunter like Wilburn Parker, the king of the Balsam bear hunters. Nor are we likely to ever see any bear dogs to match Parker's magnificent Hardwood Plott hound line. Long may they run!

CHAPTER 5
HUNTING CLUBS OF THE GREAT SMOKY MOUNTAINS

From the late 1800s through the first half of the twentieth century, hunting clubs were common in the southern Appalachians, and almost all of them played integral roles in the perpetuation of the national notoriety of the Plott breed. A few of them still exist today, although on a much smaller scale.

These early clubs generally fell into two categories: they were either owned by huge corporations that used the camps as a form of entertainment for their executives and clients or else they were privately owned by local citizens who utilized the camps for their own personal use and that of their members and friends.

Clubs that were privately owned by local citizens and businessmen were much more common in the region, but with one distinct difference. The owners of many of these clubs, all avid outdoorsmen, along with their rank-and-file members and guests, were usually affluent, prominent businessmen, doctors and lawyers. Like the larger corporate-owned clubs, they often had lodging available and service staff employed on site, along with local hunting guides and a game warden or superintendent who managed the operation.

In other instances, private local clubs catered to the rank-and-file bear hunter, common everyday working folks who just enjoyed the sport. These clubs—like the Appalachian Hunting and Fishing Club, started by the Calhoun family in the Hazel Creek Watershed—were far less formal, with more Spartan arrangements. They were strictly no frills, and usually had few, if any, employees. Typically, they consisted of good local hunters who just enjoyed hunting and fishing together, although some of them depended on the meat for their survival.

These clubs all had one thing in common: Plott hounds were generally the preferred hunting dog of the guides and hunters employed there.

Even during the depths of the Great Depression, hunting clubs flourished in the hills and hollows of the southern highlands. Thanks to their often-affluent ownership and clientele, the clubs were seldom adversely affected by the dire economy. And even the less formal groups flourished because their members *had* to hunt to feed their families, regardless of the economy. These clubs were especially popular in the Great Smoky Mountains region of Western North Carolina.

Probably the best example of the elaborate corporate hunting club was the Whiting Manufacturing Company operation on Hooper's Bald in Graham County, North Carolina. In 1908, Whiting Manufacturing bought the 5,429-foot-peak, along with a large portion of the land surrounding it.

The organization dedicated two thousand acres to a private hunting refuge and fenced in more than one thousand acres to house exotic animals shipped there from around the world—including Russian boar that would

A 1924 photo of Spence Field Hunting Cabin, with Plott dog. *Courtesy of GSMNP Archives.*

A 1937 photo of Hunting and Fishing Club, thought to have been near Cataloochee. *Courtesy of GSMNP Archives.*

A 1928 photo of Plott brothers on a bear hunt with a Graham County hunting club. Von Plott is kneeling on the far left, John Plott is kneeling on the second left and Sam Plott is standing and bending over on the far right.

later escape and become a scourge to the region. The Plott breed got its first true test of hog hunting here. By 1912, a nice lodge was open on the summit of Hooper's Bald, and the sanctuary was managed by a renowned local hunter, Garland "Cotton" McGuire.

This operation was profiled in my second book, *A History of Hunting in the Great Smoky Mountains*. By 1924, Whiting had closed the lodge. In 1926, it sold the property to Champion Paper. Champion wisely retained "Cotton" McGuire as the property manager and used the location as a lodge of its own for years after that. McGuire, a local mountain legend, lived on Hooper's Bald the remainder of his life, and his family retains land there today.

An excellent example of a privately owned club by local citizens was also in Graham County, North Carolina. It was in a rugged section of the county on Little Snowbird Creek known as Panther Flats. Until recently, I had

Panther Flats hunting camp in Graham County, North Carolina, 1906. *Courtesy of Leota Wilcox.*

always considered the Panther Flats Camp as being a communal, informal sort of club, shared equally by local hunters on public or private land—like the Appalachian Hunting and Fishing Club on Hazel Creek.

However, the Panther Flats Camp was privately owned by lawyers Marshall Bell and Jack Dillard, both of whom resided in Murphy, North Carolina. Marshall Bell was a native of Robbinsville, North Carolina, and he knew the mountains, local bear hunters and their Plott hounds well.

Bell shared a law practice in Murphy with a fellow barrister by the name of J.H. "Jack" Dillard. Dillard was a renowned criminal defense attorney and politician who was equally as well known for his love of bear hunting and Plott dogs. Both Dillard and Bell had the financial means to obtain some of the best Plott hounds and hunting grounds in the country in an area that was famous for both.

It is not clear exactly when Panther Flats first opened, but it was going strong in 1906. Newspapers across the nation—including publications in New York City, Pittsburgh, Chicago and Charlotte, among others—repeatedly published feature stories that year pertaining to bear hunting at Panther Flats, as well as an iconic Plott hound named Jude, owned by the legendary John Denton.

Denton, a Civil War veteran, was not only a famous hunter and Plott enthusiast but also equally as well known for his fighting skills. In 1892, he beat up thirty men single-handedly on the town square of Robbinsville, North Carolina, armed only with his fists, feet, some rocks and stove wood. This story and a profile of the Denton family is also included in my second book.

It is likely that both Dillard and Bell obtained their own Plott dogs from the Denton clan, who lived nearby on Little Snowbird Creek, and several members of that illustrious family were employed at Panther Flats as guides for years. The remote camp could only be accessed by horseback. It was surrounded by land teeming with wild game ranging from bear to deer and turkey, as well as various forms of small game, along with superb trout fishing.

From at least 1906 until shortly before World War II, Dillard and/or Bell entertained many of their friends and colleagues on hunting and fishing trips to Panther Flats. The lodge was sometimes known locally as the Dillard Cabin and was well known for not only its outstanding sporting opportunities but also its excellent food and drink, harvested and prepared by Pearl Yearwood.

Yearwood, sometimes spelled Earwood, was a skilled local hunter and fisherman employed by Dillard and Bell as a guide, cook and camp keeper at the Dillard Cabin. Yearwood was as adept in the kitchen and garden as he was in the woods. The fertile bottom land around the lodge produced bountiful, fresh vegetables for the hunters' dining. Yearwood once raised a fifty-six-pound head of cabbage that he sold in Marble, North Carolina, for five dollars. Good grub, magnificent hunting grounds, superb hunting guides and even better Plott hounds made Panther Flats an outstanding destination for Bell and Dillard and their friends and associates.

A similar privately owned camp of the same era was the Waynesville Rod and Gun Club, near Sunburst in Haywood County, North Carolina. I am not sure when the organization first started, but reportedly it was in the early 1900s. The club already had a fully equipped lodge in operation in 1919, and numerous local newspaper articles regularly reported on the excellent hunting and fishing there that year and for many years to follow.

The club was founded by Dr. Nick Medford along with several of his friends from Waynesville, North Carolina. Although the club has been closed for decades, the building and property are still owned by the Medford family today. Club members included notable hunters and houndsmen such as Dr. J.F. Abel and Plott family members Cody Plott, Roy Plott, Von Plott, Homer Plott and later John Plott, when he returned to the area in 1924.

Some members of the Waynesville Rod and Gun Club, including club founder Dr. Nick Medford (*top row, center, third from left*), wearing a dark plaid long-sleeved shirt. *Courtesy of Steven and Linda Rich.*

In return for free membership, several of the Plott men mentioned served as hunting guides for the club. The Plott boys also provided the services of their renowned Plott hounds for the organization, as did Wilburn Parker and his Hardwood Plott dogs. Dr. Abel's dogs, a hunting strain of hound known locally as Abel hounds, were also highly respected in the region and used at the club as well.

These canines played an important role in Plott breed history too. You can find Abel bloodlines in the pedigree of Gola Ferguson's famous Plott hounds Boss and Tige (see chapter 3 for details). There was certainly no shortage of fine hunting dogs—particularly Plott hounds—here and at all these clubs.

Another well-known hunting club in the region was the Hargrove Club at Lake Logan, North Carolina, named for the "Dean of Haywood County bear hunters," "Uncle" Joe Hargrove. He was honorary chairman of the group and served as a guide at Panther Flats and other clubs as well. The Hargrove membership roster included prominent local doctor J.L. Reeves, who served as club president, and Haywood County school superintendent A.J. Hutchins, who was vice-president.

Still other regional hunting clubs included the Deep Creek Rod and Gun Club outside Bryson City, North Carolina. It was at least partly owned by Champion Fiber, as was the Timbertop Lodge, near Indian Gap. Several local renowned hunters, including Mark Cathey, Granville Calhoun, Sam Hunnicutt and Jonah Seay, also frequented a club on Deep Creek near Bryson Place. It was owned by Bryson City attorney Thad Bryson.

The Blue Boar Lodge, near Robbinsville, North Carolina, was built by the American Aluminum Company as a retreat for its employees in 1930.

Swain County hunters at clubhouse in early 1900s. Mark Cathey is standing third from left, and Granville Calhoun is standing third from right. *Courtesy of Jim Casada.*

It would later become almost exclusively a hunting lodge where Plott breed legend Ronnie Creasman served as a guide for years, as did "Little" Will Orr before him. Recently, the Blue Boar Lodge has reverted to serve mostly as a tourist resort, but it was once renowned for its excellent fishing and hunting, especially hog hunting.

There were too many other hunting camps in the Smokies to mention them all. But the best example—and to the best of my knowledge the largest example—of a privately (or corporate) owned hunting club, was the Hazel Creek Rod and Gun Club in Swain County, North Carolina. It was located about ten miles above Proctor, North Carolina, in what is now the Great Smoky Mountains National Park or else now under the waters of Fontana Lake.

A good argument can be made that the Hazel Creek Rod and Gun Club brought more worldwide recognition to the Plott hound breed than any other club or any other historically relevant location in breed history. Not even Plott Valley, where the breed first became famous, is as well known.

Four major factors contributed to this phenomenon: the unique location and history of the Hazel Creek Watershed and club; the ownership of the club; the incredible hunting guides, as well as their even more magnificent Plott hounds; and the legendary 1935 Branch Rickey hunt. Let's briefly examine each of these categories and their impact on Plott breed history.

HAZEL CREEK WATERSHED HISTORY AND LOCATION

The Hazel Creek Watershed is located entirely in Swain County, North Carolina. It is one of three major watersheds in the southwestern part of the Great Smoky Mountains National Park. The remaining two watersheds of this region are the Eagle Creek and Forney Creek Watersheds. The Eagle Creek drainage is to the west of Hazel Creek, on the other side of Jenkins Trail Ridge, while the Forney Creek location is on the opposite side of Welch Ridge, to the east. Before the park was formed, all three watersheds were renowned as prime bear hunting locations and were home to some of the finest bear hunters and Plott hounds ever to roam the southern Appalachian range.

The headwaters of Hazel Creek originate near the lofty summit of Siler's Bald. From there, the largest stream on the North Carolina side of the Smokies flows almost eighteen miles before terminating at the mouth of the tributary, into what is now Fontana Lake. But its terminus originally emptied directly onto the Little Tennessee River, near what was formerly the now partially submerged logging town of Proctor, North Carolina.

The stream was originally named Hazelnut Creek due to the prolific number of hazel nut bushes that lined its shores. But sometime in the late 1800s, the name of the storied tributary was shortened to simply Hazel Creek.

Long before white settlers arrived in the region, Cherokee Indians maintained a small village at the confluence of Hazel Creel and Sugar Fork and enjoyed good hunting there. The tribe used an ancient network of trail systems that connected Hazel Creek to what is now known as Cades Cove and Forney Creek and to the east along the Tuckasegee River to what is now Bryson City but was once a Cherokee village, known as Big Bear's Reserve or Big Bear's Place. The most notable (and probably the oldest) of these paths was the Ekaneetlee Trace, which connected the Cherokee villages along the Little Tennessee River with tribal hunting grounds in east Tennessee.

Several Cherokee families originally lived in the narrow valley known as Pumpkin Hollow and later maintained good relationships with the first two white settlers in the region: Moses Proctor in 1829 and Samuel Cable in 1835. Andrew "Doc" Jones was another early friend to the Cherokee tribe. Jones, a native of Jackson County, North Carolina, was a notable bear hunter and Plott dog man. He moved to Hazel Creek in the early 1860s and lived there until his death in 1935. Jones is mentioned prominently as a hunter and storyteller in Horace Kephart's book *Our Southern Highlanders*. Doc Jones reportedly spoke fluent Cherokee and said that as late as the 1870s, a family of Cherokee Indians still resided on an island in the middle of Hazel Creek.

Author Horace Kephart, who lived on Hazel Creek from 1904 to 1907, deemed the region as the most rugged and isolated wilderness area east of the Mississippi River. It remains so today, and it is often referred to locally as simply the "North Shore," as it makes up the northern shore of Fontana Lake in the Great Smoky Mountains National Park. It is now accessible only by boat or foot.

However, long before Kephart's arrival, several communities were already well established along the Hazel Creek Basin. Between 1830 and 1944, all sorts of interesting communities and resourceful people dotted the Hazel Creek Watershed. But in the historical context of our hunting club story, we will focus primarily on Proctor, along with, to a lesser extent, the smaller communities of Cable Branch, Medlin and Bone Valley.

Proctor was located near the confluence of Shehan Branch and Hazel Creek. The community was named for Moses Proctor and later became a bustling lumber town in the early 1900s. It was also the jumping-off point for Hazel Creek Rod and Gun Club guests arriving by rail at the local depot, or by car, via old NC Route 288, which ran nearby.

Cable Branch—named for Sam Cable—was downstream from Proctor at the confluence of Hazel Creek and Cable Branch where Cable first settled. It was home to the Cable clan and their Cable/Plott hounds, some of the most renowned hunters and hunting hounds ever to roam the Great Smoky Mountains. Sam Cable was the iconic patriarch of the Cable family. Some of the Cable clan worked as guides at the Hazel Creek Club and occasionally provided dogs for hunts there.

Thomas Joshua Calhoun, father to the iconic Granville Calhoun, came to the region from South Carolina shortly after the Civil War. He first settled in Wayside, near Bushnell, North Carolina. Granville Calhoun was born there in 1875 but moved to Hazel Creek with his family as a boy in 1884. The Calhouns originally settled just upstream from the mouth of Bone Valley Creek.

The elder Calhoun, truly a Renaissance man, was once described as "having more interests than barley had oats—and all for good purpose." He farmed, raised a huge herd of cattle, maintained more than one hundred bee gums, ran a store, served as a Baptist preacher and started the first school on Hazel Creek, all while carving out the first wagon road into the valley.

Renowned historian and University of Tennessee professor Ken Wise described Bone Valley as "a long, narrow draw that extends from Hazel Creek to the lower slope of Thunderhead Mountain." It received its gruesome name when a herd of cattle froze to death there during a terrible blizzard in either the 1870s or 1880s. The bleached, skeletal remains of the cows reportedly remained visible to valley visitors for decades.

Left to right: Sam Sparks, Hubert Cable and Fonz Cable, with Little John Cable standing in the rear. This photo was taken in 1906 when Little John was eighty-one.

A family photo of Joshua Calhoun and clan at their Hazel Creek home in the 1880s.

Granville Calhoun inherited his father's work ethic and resourceful nature, along with a keen wit and wry sense of humor. He later became a well-known businessman in Proctor and Medlin during the timber boom of the early 1900s. Granville was also one of the finest hunters and fishermen in the region and a dedicated proponent of the Plott breed. Calhoun occasionally served as warden of the Hazel Creek Hunting Club during his varied and illustrious career. Often referred to as the "Squire of Hazel Creek," Calhoun once described hunting in the Hazel Creek Watershed like this:

> *This was great hunting country on those days. A man could hunt just about anything—bear, deer, squirrel or wild turkey. When I was young, folks that carried a rifle to get something for supper never had to come home a-suckin' the barrel! We shifted from one kind of meat to another. There was plenty of game back then, and the very best bear hunting that there ever was, was back there in the Smokies on Hazel Creek and beyond.*

On one famous hunting trip in the late 1800s, Granville reported that he and five friends harvested a wide variety of game while hunting near the Tennessee state line on Thunderhead Mountain:

> *We had the biggest bunch of game that I ever saw brought in at one time. We had eleven turkeys, a dozen squirrels, a whole raft of pheasants, a bear, a deer, a ground hog and a coon.*

The hunters eagerly looked forward to another successful outing the following day. This time, their focus was going to be solely on bears and hunting them with hounds. It turned out to be a disappointment, to say the least, as Calhoun humorously recounted:

> *The next morning we set out. We had good Plott dogs and anticipated a good bear fight. But the joke was on us. We never saw a single bear or even turned a dog loose. We never even heard one in the brush. We didn't kill a thing that day. I reckon word got passed around among the bears and other animals that a bunch of true shooters was in the mountains and they all high-tailed it for parts unknown and holed in.*

Horace Kephart reported in 1904 that Medlin, a small community at the confluence of Hazel Creek and Sugar Fork established by Marion Medlin in the early 1860s, consisted of "two small stores—one owned by the Calhoun clan—a post office, a corn mill and two private residences." Medlin was the nearest community to the Hazel Creek Club.

Residents of the Hazel Creek Watershed led largely self-sufficient lives. They raised their own crops and livestock and supplemented their diets with healthy amounts of locally harvested fish and game. What they couldn't grow, kill or make, they bought or traded for at various general stores in the region or else went into the town of Bryson City for larger purchases if needed.

It was a simple and hard but satisfying lifestyle for Hazel Creek mountaineers, who loved their freedom. Hunting and dogs—especially Plott hounds—played integral roles in their culture throughout the nineteenth century and well into the twentieth. That all changed with the logging and mining boom of the early 1900s—in some ways for better but in more ways for the worse.

As early as 1888, timber agents, like Jack Coburn, arrived in the region to acquire mineral and timber rights for major timber companies, such as the Ritter, Montvale, Ravensford and Champion Fiber logging companies. Coburn eventually owned shares in several mining and logging companies in the Hazel Creek Watershed, most notably with Ritter Lumber and J.P. Stikeleather's logging and mining operations. Coburn later had a home near the mouth of Bone Valley Creek.

Ritter Lumber Company and the R.E. Woods Company were the earliest logging operations to utilize railroad utilities to transport the timber to market. Ritter built its own railroad line eighteen miles up Hazel Creek in 1902, with spur lines to Sugar Fork, Bone Valley and Walker Creek. The Ritter line was known as the Smoky Mountain Railroad and

A boy hunting with a flintlock in what is now the GSMNP in early 1900s. Note the huge chestnut stump behind him. *Courtesy of GSMNP Archives.*

connected with the main Southern Railway line at the Ritter Lumber Mill in Proctor.

By 1907, Montvale Lumber was going strong on Eagle Creek, and Ritter Lumber was setting production records in Proctor by 1910. This resulted in a population boom and all sorts of business opportunities, which renowned bear hunter Granville Calhoun wisely took advantage of.

Ritter Lumber Company in Proctor, North Carolina, about 1912.

The Squire of Hazel Creek expanded his business holdings beyond Medlin to acquire another store in Proctor, along with at least seventeen various parcels of real estate, as well as Proctor's first movie theater. Nevertheless, Calhoun knew that the influx of lumber companies, followed later by the formation of the Great Smoky Mountains National Park and Fontana Lake, meant the beginning of the end to his idyllic sporting life on Hazel Creek. Or, as he so eloquently put it:

> *Then came the lumber men. Why it was just like a revolution, and I guess it was. It changed the valley. Folks who understood a rifle trigger and a fishing pole saw things they had never heard of, much less seen. There wasn't much time left for hunting and fishing.*

Calhoun was absolutely correct in his assessment. But fortunately, the logging boom ended almost as quickly as it began. By 1927, Ritter Lumber had sold the bulk of its holdings in the Hazel Creek Watershed and, for all practical purposes, had ceased operations. Stikeleather Lumber Company closed soon after that. Only Champion Fiber and Ravensford remained in operation in 1929. Both fiercely contested the formation of the GSMNP and continued operating until the park was officially chartered by Congress in 1934.

Writer Horace Kephart revisited his former Hazel Creek home at the height of the logging boom and was devastated by what he saw. He described this once pristine wilderness as now being "wrecked, ruined, desecrated and vile and mean." Just as his friend Granville Calhoun stated, a revolution had indeed taken place—albeit one with intensely adverse results to the Hazel Creek Basin and its residents.

However, all was not lost for bear hunting with Plott dogs in the Hazel Creek Watershed. With the lumber industry essentially dead by 1927 and the Great Depression looming on the horizon, many Hazel Creek residents found themselves without a means of income.

Granville Calhoun sitting on the porch of his store in Proctor, North Carolina.

After spending almost two decades working as loggers or miners, they were forced to return to the old ways. They had to in order to survive. Bear hunting again became essential to their survival, both in putting meat on the table and as a means of employment by working as guides for the corporate clubs.

Moreover, it would still be about a decade before Hazel Creek residents would be forced to relocate by the Park Service and Tennessee Valley Authority. And even then, hunting was still allowed in the Hazel Creek Watershed until at least 1944, more than four years after President Roosevelt officially dedicated the park in 1940.

Indeed, one can argue that the period between 1924 and 1944 comprised the glory years of bear hunting with Plott hounds in the Hazel Creek Watershed, at least regarding the nationwide publicity generated by the various hunting clubs and their members scattered across the southern highlands. Plott breed legend Wilburn Parker described the Hazel Creek Watershed in 1933 as a "bear hunter's paradise."

And it all began, in large part, due to the formation of the Hazel Creek Hunting Club, headquartered one mile upstream from the mouth of Bone Valley Creek on the east side of Hazel Creek, and to a much lesser degree, the Kress Hunting Lodge, near the site of the Crate Hall Cabin, located at the mouth of Bone Valley Creek.

The owners of the Hazel Creek Club and the size of this massive piece of property are as intriguing as the colorful history of the watershed. They are the second reason why the club and the region hold such a special place in the legacy of the Plott breed.

CLUB OWNERS AND LAND ACQUISITION

One of the last lumber companies operating in the Hazel Creek Watershed was Stikeleather Lumber Company, owned by affluent Asheville, North Carolina businessman and sportsman J.G. "Jim" Stikeleather. Stikeleather was an avid fly fisherman and hunter. He frequented the Hazel Creek region often—both for business and pleasure.

The Stikeleather operation had logged all over the Smokies, generating high profits for its owner. Stikeleather also owned other successful businesses as well, including a copper mine located at the head of Hazel Creek in which he shared ownership with Jack Coburn and Doc Jones. Stikeleather's business and personal interests further resulted in the formation of the Hazel Creek Rod and Gun Club.

The exact club charter date is not known, but as the logging boom came an to end, J.P. Stikeleather and his partners began to acquire large parcels of land for their own private fishing and hunting sanctuary. It was originally known as simply the Hazel Creek Fishing Club. Over the next two decades, the club would be referred to by many names, including the Hazel Creek Rod and Gun Club, the Hazel Creek Hunting Club, the Hazel Creek Hunting and Fishing Club, the Stikeleather-Smathers Club and, more often, simply as the Hazel Creek Clubhouse.

Writer Jim Gasque, author of the classic 1948 book *Hunting and Fishing in the Great Smoky Mountains*, was Jim Stikeleather's nephew. Gasque spent more than twenty years fishing at the club. Gasque wrote that in the early 1920s, his uncle and a group of other Western North Carolina sportsmen became "possessors of a vast boundary of land" on Hazel Creek. The author recalled that he took his first trip to the club in 1924, so we know for sure the club was operating by then.

From his days managing his business operations, Stikeleather knew the Hazel Creek Basin intimately, and along with his partners, he continued to acquire additional acreage for the club up until at least 1928 and probably longer. By 1928, according to historian and writer Don Casada—and further verified by Swain County deed books—Stikeleather and his partners had acquired almost 23,000 acres of prime hunting property in the Hazel Creek Watershed (22,792 acres to be exact). Another 214 acres were in dispute, so the grand total was a little over 23,000 acres.

However, Hazel Creek guide Oliver Laws estimated in a 1985 interview that the club had hunting access to 105,000 acres by 1935, or about 164 square miles of prime hunting land. Assuming Laws was correct, this included property the club owned, plus land surrounding its acreage deep into the Eagle Creek and Forney Creek Watersheds, as well as property along Lands Creek. Today, the entire GSMNP consists of about 520,000 acres, so this provides a better perspective of the massive proportions of the Hazel Creek Club.

While I don't know for sure the total price the owners originally paid for the land, historian and author Jim Casada's assessment that the club likely paid "bargain basement Depression era prices" for the acreage is undoubtedly correct. I would be surprised if it paid more than two dollars per acre and almost certainly not more than five dollars per acre. It was an extraordinary business deal.

To better illustrate the magnitude of the transaction, consider that when the Hazel Creek Club property was eventually sold to the Park Service in 1931 along with additional tracts sold later to the TVA, the grand total of the sale was a little over $262,000, or about $11 per acre, for twenty-three thousand acres. That is a huge return on its original investment, as the club at the very least doubled the original purchase price. Plus, keep in mind that Stikeleather's timber company had already made good money off the very same property from the logging operation.

These Western North Carolina native sportsmen were clearly very astute businessmen, and they were equally as passionate about their hunting and fishing pursuits.

Jim Stikeleather and his good friends W.M. Smathers and P.H. Branch were designated as primary club and property trustees. As trustees, the trio held the land for the benefit of the grantors with stated interest portions; all three men were both grantors and grantees of the property and were obviously leaders of the operation.

However, there were multiple other minority owners as well, most of them also well-known businessmen in Buncombe and Haywood Counties.

Prominent members included Bob Haynes, CEO of Wachovia Bank and Trust in Asheville; D. Hiden Ramsey, vice-president of the *Asheville Citizen Times* newspaper; *Citizen Times* sports editor Paul Jones; and Dr. Frank Smathers of Waynesville, just to name a few.

With the land purchased, the trustees contracted a lodge to be built sometime in the early 1920s, if not before—Gasque said that it was already there in 1924. The building—typically referred to as the Hazel Creek Clubhouse or the Stikeleather-Smathers Clubhouse—was located one mile upstream from the mouth of Bone Valley Creek, on the east bank of Hazel Creek. The clubhouse was a massive, two-story poplar log structure with multiple fireplaces and a dog trot cooking kitchen.

Yet another large hunting lodge—in this case a corporately owned operation—was later built nearby. S.H. Kress, the wealthy owner of the nationwide chain of retail stores, opened a lodge of his own here in 1940. Kress was reportedly a relative of Jesse "Crate" Hall, an early Hazel Creek settler who built his first cabin at the mouth of Bone Valley Creek in 1877 and a second one in 1892. The Kress Lodge stood within fifty yards of the Hall Cabin about one mile east-northeast of the mouth of Bone Valley on the east side of Hazel Creek. The Hall Cabin would later be used as a guesthouse for the lodge.

The Kress Lodge was a fine structure and staffed with a chef and expert wait staff. Historian Ken Wise described it as a "large, ornately appointed house" built by the Kress family on land leased to them by the Calhoun family. To the best of my knowledge, the Kress Lodge was less a hunting or fishing club as much as it was a wilderness retreat for Kress family members, friends and associates to relax and be pampered. Some guests likely did some hunting and fishing, but never on the same scale as the Hazel Creek Club.

Either way, the impact of the Kress Lodge was short-lived. By 1944, the lodge had closed after the lease was canceled by the TVA with the formation of Fontana Dam and Lake. The beautiful building was burned to the ground by vandals in the late 1940s.

I mistakenly wrote in the past that there are no remnants of either lodge remaining above water today. That is incorrect. Remains of the foundation of the Hazel Creek Clubhouse, as well as the driveway to the lodge, are still clearly visible today, as is the foundation and chimney of the Kress Lodge. However, it was the Hazel Creek Lodge that had the most impact on the Plott breed and is the focal point of our story.

Legendary hunting guide Jim Laws, father of Oliver Laws, was employed by the Hazel Creek Club as its lead game warden and guide. He was paid

Left: Hazel Creek Lodge in 1947. *Courtesy of GSMNP Archives.*

Below: Crate Hall Cabin. *Courtesy of GSMNP Archives.*

forty dollars a month and charged with not only acting as a guide when needed but also patrolling the property and evicting non-members or any other uninvited trespassers. Oliver Laws and other guides were paid thirty-five dollars monthly for their services.

The Laws family lived in a cabin directly across from the lodge on the west side of Hazel Creek. Most of the other guides were seasonal and bunked in the lodge when needed or else lived in nearby mountain communities.

All the club members, especially the trustees, had a vast network of business associates, many of whom enjoyed hunting and fishing. They included such renowned celebrities as future baseball Hall of Famer Branch Rickey, as well as acclaimed writer John Taintor Foote, along with a host of nationally known politicians, newspapermen, military men, doctors, lawyers and captains of industry.

When these guests of the Hazel Creek Club—and, to a lesser degree, the Kress Lodge—returned to their homes in various locations across the United

States, word soon spread about the fine hunting and fishing to be found in the Great Smoky Mountains. Moreover, because of their endorsements—as well as through the hunting stories printed nationally by outdoor writers like Horace Kephart, Jim Gasque, John Foote, Raymond Camp, D. Hiden Ramsey, Paul Jones and Jack Ruffing—the Plott hound, their owners and guides all gained nationwide notoriety as well.

It seems somewhat ironic that many of the men who played a large part in ravaging the Hazel Creek Watershed through their logging and mining ventures still loved the area and played an integral role in bringing nationwide recognition to the Great Smoky Mountains and to the Plott hound breed. Perhaps this was because they were all natives to the region, and as such, they still appreciated the beauty and natural resources of their homeland—it's hard to say for sure.

However, it is safe to say that the Hazel Creek Club's success was due at least in small part to the iconic Plott hounds and their equally illustrious owners and hunting guides. Without them, the owners and their guests would have had little success in following the trail of the wily black bear.

But to be fair, the Plott dogs and their owners would have likely remained a regional phenomenon had it not been for the national publicity generated by the affluent Hazel Creek Club members and their guests. Let's look at some of the club's better-known guides.

Hazel Creek Guides

With strong ownership, a vast amount of prime private hunting land, a well-staffed lodge, expert guides and superb Plott bear hounds, all the pieces were in place for the Hazel Creek Rod and Gun Club's success. These components were all equally important, but it is fair to say that the guides and Plott dogs were the cornerstones of the club's success. And a large part of that success began with club superintendent James Nelson Laws, better known as "Uncle" Jim Laws.

Jim oversaw the entire operation, but several other individuals, including Wilburn Parker, were responsible for policing specific sections of the club to prevent poaching. Parker was well known in the region for his hunting skills and outstanding Plott hounds.

Although there were reportedly several club superintendents over the years, including Granville Calhoun, Jim Laws was the only one who lived at the club full time and enjoyed the longest tenure in the job, apparently well over two decades, starting in about 1920. Jim's son, Oliver Laws, was first employed by the club as a guide in 1930.

Other notable club guides worthy of mention—all fiercely dedicated Plott hound advocates—were Von Plott, "Little" George Plott, brothers Taylor and Kay Wilson, Mark Cathey, Wince Cable, Reggie Enloe, Bill Wiggins, Gola Ferguson and Cody Plott.

Plott breed legend Steve Fielder arranged for an interview with Oliver Laws in 1985. Through that interview, as well as information found in Plott family archives, various nationally published articles and books, along with interviews I have personally conducted, we have a good deal of information about the Laws family, the lodge, the other Hazel Creek guides and their dogs.

The elder Laws reportedly killed more than one hundred bears in his hunting career, as did his son, Oliver. Jim kept a laurel stick with a notch carved in it for every bear harvested. Baseball Hall of Famer Branch Rickey noticed in 1935 that Jim Laws had killed many of these bruins with an old shotgun that had a slightly crooked barrel.

Rickey referred to Jim Laws by the honorary mountain term of endearment of "Uncle" Jim and asked Laws if perhaps it was time for a new gun. Laws replied, "What for? I can still get a good shot with it as long as I aim it right." Rickey later had new engraved Winchester hunting rifles sent to Laws and all the Hazel Creek guides as gifts.

A 1935 photo of iconic Hazel Creek guides and Plott dog men (*left to right*) Reg Enloe, Oliver Laws, Jim Laws and Von Plott.

Above: A 1935 photo of Hazel Creek guides, clients and Plott hounds at Hazel Creek Clubhouse. Little George Plott is kneeling on ground at far left, Von Plott is standing at far left, Jim Laws is hatless standing to right of chimney and Mark Cathey is to his left wearing a hat.

Right: Hazel Creek guide Oliver Laws, with rifle given to him by Branch Rickey.

Jim Laws and his son were both avid Plott dog men and close friends with the Plott family and breed icon Gola Ferguson. Oliver Laws said that his father obtained his first Plott hounds directly from Von Plott. Laws later received additional Plott hounds from a Knoxville lawyer who had acquired his first Plott dogs from Von Plott in 1925.

Laws vividly recalled seeing John Plott's famous Plott hound Plott's Lep hunt at the club, along with "Little" George Plott's storied buckskin Plott that was named either Buck or Buckskin, depending on the source. He remembered all the dogs listed on the 1935 Rickey hunt as well. Laws added that he was especially impressed with Von Plott's legendary hound Scott, a black saddleback with bold brindle trim that was whelped in 1931. "He was the best Plott dog of them all!" Laws exclaimed.

Oliver Laws and "Little" George Plott were about the same age—Plott was twenty-three in 1935—and Laws said that they were best friends. Laws believed that Little George was the best of all the guides and added, "Little George was a real sport, Von may have been a better hunter, but he was a lot older and Little George wasn't far behind him even then. Branch Rickey once said that me, Von and Little George were the runningest bear hunters he had ever seen."

The Wilson brothers, Taylor and Kay, lived near the Plott family in Haywood County. They, too, were similar in age to both Oliver Laws and "Little" George Plott and were also close friends to both, as well as superb Hazel Creek guides.

The Wilson boys began their hunting careers as diehard advocates of the black and tan breed but soon saw the light and switched over to Plott hounds. Taylor Wilson, in particular, was very well known for his outstanding Plott dogs. He once killed a bear armed only with a knife as his Plott dogs bayed the beast on a Hazel Creek hunt in 1936.

Laws's accounts of several of his Hazel Creek adventures with "Little" George Plott are described in detail in my third book, *Legendary Hunters of the Southern Highlands*. Laws was rightfully impressed with his heroic friend, Captain George Ellis Plott, who was killed in action in World War II. (Jack Edwards also offers additional insight on Captain Plott and their boyhood together in chapter 6.)

Gola Ferguson, former sheriff of Swain County, is widely regarded as one of the top five most important men in early Plott breed history—the others being John A. Plott, Von Plott, Isaiah Kidd and Taylor Crockett. Of this so-called Big Five, we know that three of them—Von, John and Gola—all served as guides at the Hazel Creek Club and provided their respective Plott dogs for hunting. It is generally believed that Taylor Crockett hunted there as well.

Alec (or Alex) Taylor was yet another highly esteemed Hazel Creek guide, and like the Wilson brothers, he was a good friend of the Plott family. He had a stellar reputation for his own Plott hounds, originally obtained from the Plott clan, and he owned three of the seventeen dogs on the 1935 Rickey hunt.

Wince Cable—a member of the famous Cable hunting clan—and Bill Wiggins were both well-known guides, and both were directly related to the Laws family, while Wiggins was kin to the Plott family, too. Reggie "Reg" Enloe of Sylva, North Carolina, regularly served as a dog handler and guide on Hazel Creek as well. He was a good friend of Von Plott's and hunted with him often, as well as Wilburn Parker.

Club guide Mark Cathey is rightly regarded as the best all-around sportsman in the annals of Smoky Mountain field and stream history. Due to his prolific combination of world-class hunting and fishing skills, Cathey quite simply had no peer in this regard. He was a master of all forms of hunting and fishing and a diehard Plott hound man. Cathey's renowned storytelling skills and wry sense of humor matched his talents as a hunting and fishing guide.

However, as far as strictly bear hunting with hounds, the most famous of the Hazel Creek bear hunting guides, and arguably the best of the group, was probably H.V. "Von" Plott of Waynesville, North Carolina. Plott was born in 1896 and was in his hunting prime during the glory days of the Hazel Creek Rod and Gun Club in the 1930s and early '40s. You can read a complete profile of Von Plott in my fourth book, *Colorful Characters of the Great Smoky Mountains.*

Plott had taken over the family Plott hound pack from his father, Montraville Plott, in about 1920 and later became world famous for his contributions to the breed. A lot of that notoriety began with his work as a Hazel Creek guide. Plott had guided for many clubs in the Smokies, but he fondly recalled to writer Jerry Dyer in 1972 that the Hazel Creek Club was his favorite:

> *We had hunting lodges all over the mountains back then. The one that I favored most was up on Hazel Creek near the Tennessee state line. About fifty men would be there at a time from all over the country. The most famous hunt was the Rickey hunt in 1935. My dogs treed every bear on that hunt, but they were always doing that. Bears were never a problem for our dogs. I remember another big hunt in 1936 when we jumped some hogs*

Left: Mark Cathey and dog.

Below: Von Plott pointing out bear sign to a friend.

on Hazel Creek—and the fight was on! A Plott hound will stand their ground right along with the hunter—IF he will. My dogs like to have a little company in the fight and I make sure that they have it.

Before his death in 1979, Von Plott had hunted bear behind his famous dogs in locations ranging from almost every part of the Great Smokies to the North Carolina coastal plain, as far north as Michigan and as far west as Texas and Colorado. He would play a large role in the Plott breed being officially recognized by the United Kennel Club in 1946 and is widely considered the most iconic figure in Plott breed history.

Despite all these well-deserved accolades and fond hunting memories, Von Plott cherished his days working as a guide on Hazel Creek above all others. The 1935 Rickey hunt was his all-time favorite hunting experience, and not just because it was a record-setting hunt.

Instead, Plott placed more value on seeing his friend Branch Rickey kill two bears while hunting behind Von and his celebrated Plott hounds. We'll review the Rickey hunt and the Plott dogs involved in detail shortly. But first let's take a brief look at the remarkable life of Branch Rickey, a man Von Plott considered a treasured friend the remainder of his life, as well as how Rickey became an integral part of Plott breed history almost by accident.

BRANCH RICKEY, RENAISSANCE MAN

Branch Rickey personified the definition of a true Renaissance man. It is a term that is often overused in attempting to describe individuals who are experts in multiple fields or who excel in many different areas. But in the case of Branch Rickey, the term fits perfectly, as Rickey not only led an extraordinary life but also literally changed history in the process.

Branch Rickey was an accomplished athlete and scholar. He played college and professional baseball, as well as professional football, and he obtained a law degree from the University of Michigan, where he also began his baseball coaching career. His baseball career was interrupted from 1917 through 1918 while he served as an officer in the U.S. Army fighting on the Western Front in France during World War I.

Rickey could have taken a multitude of career paths after his military service. But baseball was his true passion. Including his service before and after the war, Rickey devoted more than half a century of his life to the betterment of the sport.

During his storied career as a baseball executive, Branch Rickey won seven National League titles and five world championships with the Cardinals, while also leading the Brooklyn Dodgers to two pennants. Rickey is credited with the origination and development of the minor-league baseball farm system, in which talent was developed for the major leagues. In 1953, he revolutionized safety standards in the big leagues when he developed and implemented the use of batting helmets while serving as the general manager for the Pittsburgh Pirates.

As impressive as all these accomplishments were, they pale in comparison to the courage Rickey demonstrated when he integrated professional baseball in 1945 by signing the sport's first African American player, Jackie Robinson, to a contract with the Brooklyn Dodgers. This was a decision that literally revolutionized professional sports in America and affected United States history as well.

Jackie Robinson would later join Rickey as baseball Hall of Fame members, as did many other players he drafted and developed, such as Dizzy Dean, Enos Slaughter, Roberto Clemente and Stan Musial. Hall of Fame sportswriter Jim Murray, remarking on Rickey's keen eye for recognizing talent, once said that Rickey could "recognize a great player from the window of a moving train."

After developing the minor-league farm system in 1919, Rickey considered moving his St. Louis Cardinal farm club from Greensboro, North Carolina, to Asheville, North Carolina, in 1934. He visited the Western North Carolina city in 1934 and called Asheville's McCormick Field "the prettiest ball park in the world."

Rickey became friends with local businessmen and prominent citizens such as Hazel Creek Rod and Gun Club members W.P. Smathers, J.P. Stikeleather and D. Hiden Ramsey. They convinced Rickey to move his team to Asheville for the 1935 season. The trio also first introduced Rickey to bear hunting with Plott hounds at the Hazel Creek Club.

Even after Rickey left the Cardinals, he remained close to his Asheville friends and personally helped the city acquire a Dodgers farm team in 1946. This team became known as the Asheville Tourists and later served as a farm club for the Pirates while Rickey was employed in Pittsburgh. The Tourists remain in operation today at McCormick Field as a Class A affiliate of the Colorado Rockies.

D. Hiden Ramsey and Rickey were especially close friends. Ramsey, a newspaper executive in Asheville and prominent Hazel Creek Club member, hunted and fished with Rickey often, in Western North Carolina as well as Canada. Ramsey spoke fondly of Rickey, calling him "a man of deep religious convictions, just one of the most wonderful personalities I have ever known."

Ramsey further added, "Branch loved the outdoors. He was an excellent rifle shot and a fair fly fisherman. He loved the mountains of western North Carolina. He was an incomparable storyteller, a man of tremendous vitality, who could sit up all night spinning yarns and then be the first man up the next morning."

However, to fully comprehend the scope of Rickey's celebrity status and the impact he had in bringing nationwide notoriety to the Plott breed, one must appreciate Rickey's relevance in the sporting world of that era. Unlike today, when the National Football League rules supreme as the most popular sport in America, professional baseball, followed closely by pro boxing and horse racing, were far and away the nation's most popular spectator sports during the first half of the twentieth century.

The fact that Branch Rickey worked for two of the most popular teams in the sport, and later had part ownership in one of them, along with his incredible winning records with the Cardinals franchise and later with the Dodgers and Pirates, vaulted Rickey into a stellar celebrity universe. Rickey's notoriety was similar in many ways to athletes such as Babe Ruth, Jack Dempsey or Jack Johnson by 1935. His every move was noted daily in newspapers and magazines across the nation.

To have someone of this status personally affiliated with the Plott hound breed and a hunting club in Western North Carolina was unheard of. Titans of industry, famous regional and national politicians and captains of the business world were no strangers to the Hazel Creek Club; indeed, even the club owners were well known nationwide. But Branch Rickey's involvement took this recognition to an entirely different level—for the region, the club and the Plott breed.

It is not known how many times Rickey hunted and fished at the Hazel Creek Club. Although based on numerous reports and interviews, as well as his time spent conducting business in the area, the impression conveyed is that Rickey was a frequent visitor to the sanctuary. However, we know for sure that Rickey was hunting at the club in October 1935. It would prove to be a hunt for the ages—unlike any other, before or since.

THE 1935 BRANCH RICKEY HAZEL CREEK HUNT

The 1935 Branch Rickey Hazel Creek Hunt was legendary for several reasons: the involvement of Branch Rickey, the number of expert guides in attendance and the large number of bears harvested in only two days by seventeen world-class Plott hounds. Now, let's take a closer look at the actual event and the Plott hounds that participated in this classic 1935 hunt.

Rickey's specific arrival date to the club is not certain, nor can we verify if this was his first trip there. However, we know for sure that he was present on the two biggest days of the hunt (October 20 and October 21, 1935), when the guides and their Plott hounds jumped twenty bears and killed eight in less than forty-eight hours—six on the twentieth and two on the twenty-first.

Thanks to Plott breed icon C.E. "Bud Lyon," who had the foresight to gather this information while many of the participants were still alive, we know more specifics about the Plott dogs involved in this illustrious event. There were seventeen legendary Plott hounds on this hunt, which began on October 20, 1935. Eleven of them were owned by Von Plott: Scott, Dan, Sunshine, Fannie, Lady, Drum, Bess, Hardwood, Mack, Kate and Betty. Three hounds were owned by John Plott and his son Little George Plott: Bute, Buckskin and Queen. The remaining three hounds—Stroll, Rush and Jake—were all owned by Alec Taylor.

Von Plott offered insight into the hunt and the Plott hounds. Following are some additional observations about the dogs: Scott was out of Boss and Lady and born in 1931. Scott was a beautiful black saddleback with bold, brindle-colored legs and trim. He was a great strike dog, fast and a good sticker. Scott was a hard fighter and a good tree dog. Jim Laws described Scott as Von's best dog ever. In a later letter to Von Plott in December 1935, Branch Rickey mentioned Scott as being one of two exceptionally impressive dogs on the hunt worthy of note. Scott carried some Blevins blood in his pedigree and was used repeatedly in Von Plott's breeding program. (See chapter 3.)

Dan was also out of Boss and Lady and a younger brother to Scott. He was whelped in 1931. Scott was very fast, a good sticker, a hard fighter and a great tree dog. And like his brother, he carried some Blevins blood. He, too, was often utilized in Von's breeding program.

Buckskin—as his name implied—was a buckskin-colored Plott, bred in 1933 by Von Plott but later owned by Little George Plott and, eventually, Sam Plott, Von's brother. Little George Plott told Jim Laws that Buckskin, or Buck, as he was often called, was his all-time best strike dog. He was out

Von Plott (*left*) with Jake Nichols and famous Plott hounds (*left to right*) Plott's Jenny, Link, Belle, Drum, Happy, Balsam, John and Roxie.

A 1935 photo of the Rickey hunt on Hazel Creek. Branch Rickey is third from the right, and Von Plott is second from the right.

of Tige and Bess and was said to be a very hard fighter and a great tree dog and renowned for his exceptional speed. There are numerous other stories about this iconic buckskin dog that was renowned for his fierce tenacity. Buck was killed by a bear in 1938, and Sam Plott wrote a story about the incident for an early NPHA yearbook.

Mack, Bute and Jake were also on the hunt. Bute was owned by Little George Plott and shows up repeatedly in future famous registered pedigrees. Few specific comments were made about Mack and Jake, although they were obviously fine dogs.

Drum was a litter mate to Trigg Plott. Drum was another exceptional dog that was mentioned specifically to Von Plott in the Rickey letter. Rickey felt strongly that Drum and Scott were the best dogs there, which is saying a lot.

Hardwood was another fierce fighter produced by Scott and Fannie. Hardwood also had some Parker family bloodlines in his pedigree, dating back to Wilburn Parker, who partnered often with the Plott family in their breeding program.

Rush, yet another male, was also known for his fierce tenacity and grit. Rush never gave up, and he never backed down—a prototypical Plott hound.

Sunshine, in some reports, was a female, while others say a male. The dog was born in 1933 out of Tige and Bess and was a sibling of Buckskin. Sunshine was an all-around fine bear dog and was renowned for multiple skill sets.

The rest of the dogs on this list, like Sunshine, were all female Plotts. They included Fannie, Queen, Lady, Kate, Bess, Betty and Stroll. They were all notable dogs, especially Kate, a fierce buckskin Plott with a keen nose. Queen was one of the three dogs on the hunt owned by Little George Plott. She was said to have been an exceptionally cold-nosed dog that could strike even the oldest and coldest of tracks. Queen was out of Buckskin and Rush.

It is also worth pointing out that of the seventeen dogs on the hunt, eight were males and nine were females—an almost even 50-50 split between the two genders. Over the years, Plott enthusiasts have debated their preference of one gender versus another as their hunting dogs of choice.

But this hunt, which was incredibly important due to Rickey's involvement, tells me that *only* the very best dogs available would have been included on the trip. The fact that they are almost evenly split by gender indicates to me that these seasoned hunters cared about only one thing: performance. Gender or coat color did *not* matter. These men were just looking for the best performing dogs. The fact that there were no other dogs on this hunt but purebred Plott hounds further validates the stellar and well-deserved reputation that the breed had rightfully earned. In the world of big game hunting, Rickey expected the best—and that's exactly what he got.

Almost all these dogs show up in the pedigrees of the first Plott hounds officially registered by the UKC in 1946. These hounds were among the foundation stock of the very first Plott dogs registered, and as such, they were directly responsible for the existence of the Plott breed today. This, too, is yet another significant element involving the Hazel Creek Club and, more specifically, the 1935 Rickey hunt.

One of the best actual firsthand accounts of the hunt comes from Von Plott. Plott described one of the many bear races to outdoor writer Jerry Dyer in 1972:

> *The dogs struck a bear and run it straight down to the car parking lot in front of the lodge—we called it the honky tonkin' place. The bear went in and out amidst the cars with everybody hollering, jumping and hoping for a shot. The bear piled off into the creek and Rickey put the power to it—he shot it with his big shotgun and broke its leg. But the bear was still fighting the dogs, so I waded out in the creek and laid open its throat with my knife. I heard Rickey a hollering, bring me some more ammo—he's a charging! I told him the bear wouldn't be charging no more.*

Oliver Laws also offered his account in a 1985 interview. He agreed that six bears were killed on the hunt, but he maintained that he killed two, while Rickey, Reg Enloe, Bob Haynes and Von Plott all harvested one bear each. Laws further added that he killed the biggest of the six bruins and that it weighed in at more than four hundred pounds. However, every other account of the hunt indicates that it was Branch Rickey—not Laws—who killed two bears, while the other members and guides listed all tallied one each. Esteemed writer Jim Gasque further confirmed this. With all due respect to Oliver Laws, perhaps his memory was fading some in 1985, or else he was just guilty of embellishing his hunting tale—as many hunters so often do.

The actual individual totals are irrelevant, as the hunt was a monumental success. Reports of the event were recorded in newspapers across the country. On December 5, 1935, Rickey sent Von Plott a letter regarding the hunt. The letter, written on St. Louis Cardinals letterhead, reads in part:

> *I shall never forget your ability to run as fast as your dogs—or almost as fast. Everyone agrees that you ran more than twelve miles that morning up and down those mountains; and at every crossing and across every hillcrest*

you were never seen to be walking—you were always running. You are what I call a finished hunter. And I think, I would rather go hunting with you in charge of the dogs than anyone else in the world.

Rickey continued his letter by pointing out how he was especially impressed with Little George Plott and how the young man was destined for great things in whatever field he chose. Mr. Rickey was absolutely correct in that assessment, too. As writer Jim Murray once said, Rickey indeed had a keen eye in evaluating talent.

Branch concluded his letter by complimenting the Plott dogs on the hunt, naming Von's dog, Scott, specifically, and reminding Von that he would still like to buy one of Alec Taylor's Plott hounds. Clearly the hunt had left a lasting impression on Rickey.

It is not known if Rickey ever obtained his own Plott hound or if he hunted at the club again, although I think he did. Regardless, Rickey's October 1935 hunt would go down in Plott breed history as the most important hunt conducted in the Great Smoky Mountains, and it would prove to be the most noteworthy event in the illustrious history of the Hazel Creek Rod and Gun Club as well. However, at what appeared to be the peak of the club's popularity, the glory days of the club were rapidly coming to an end.

The End of an Era

The 1935 Rickey hunt epitomized the height of popularity of bear hunting with Plott hounds in the Hazel Creek Watershed, and indeed at the club itself. Subsequent successful hunting and fishing trips would be enjoyed by members and their guests for several more years, including a huge bear hunt in December 1941 that was documented in a feature article in the Sunday, January 4, 1942 issue of the *Asheville Citizen Times*.

No fewer than seven Plott family members and their renowned Plott hounds served as guides on the hunt. They included Von Plott, Herbert Plott Jr., Cody Plott, Homer Plott, Big George Plott, John Plott and Little George Plott. Three of the Plott boys were home on military leave, as they were already in the army training for action in World War II at Fort Jackson, South Carolina. The Plott clan was joined by other guides, including Mark Cathey, Jim and Oliver Laws and Taylor Wilson.

These mountain hunting icons served as guides for a host of big-city guests, including Senator William Smathers of New Jersey. The hunt was a resounding success, as the group harvested three big bears—all weighing more than three hundred pounds on the outing. Sadly, it would prove to be the last bear hunt for Captain George Ellis Plott, as he was later killed in the war.

At what would seem to have been the club's peak of popularity, the truth was that it was the beginning of the end of an era. Club owners had already sold off much of the property to the National Park Service in 1931, and the rest would be sold to the Tennessee Valley Authority to build Fontana Dam and Fontana Lake a few years later.

Club owners still retained access to the lodge along with limited hunting and fishing rights—even in the GSMNP—until at least 1944, and some reports indicate possibly as late as 1946. The Park Service eventually took full control of the property then and either dismantled or burned the lodge after briefly using it as a ranger station of some sort. But for all practical purposes, the final curtain dropped on the club in 1944.

Guide Oliver Laws said that Branch Rickey and banker Bob Haynes—two of the club's more famous guests and members—were both devastated to learn of the club's closing. But none was more heartbroken than the iconic Mark Cathey. It seems somehow appropriate that the demise and end of hunting in the Hazel Creek Watershed would coincide with the death of Mark Cathey, the most popular guide at the Hazel Creek Club and probably the best all-around Great Smoky Mountain sportsman who ever lived.

Cathy was in declining health in the summer of 1944. A lifelong bachelor, Cathey had devoted most of his life to the mastery of hunting and fishing. In his later years, he split his time living with his sisters, Mrs. Charlie Beck, on Hughes Branch, and Mrs. Forest McCracken of Galbreath Creek—both locations outside Bryson City.

Fearing that the end was near for their beloved brother and knowing that Mark had spent little time in church, the sisters arranged for Cathey to meet with a local minister and make his final peace with God. Upon conclusion of the meeting, all parties involved agreed that their mission had been accomplished. Mark Cathey could surely pass safely through the pearly gates of Heaven upon his passing.

Shortly after that meeting, Hazel Creek Club owner Jim Stikeleather invited his old friend to accompany him on a fishing trip to Hazel Creek during the last week of August 1944. Stikeleather was aware of Cathey's declining health and wanted to honor him with a final farewell outing. Mark evidently sensed the end was nigh as well. According to writer Jim Gasque, Cathey put on a stellar fly-fishing demonstration for his friends before landing one final fish. Cathey then turned to Stikeleather and handed him the rod, saying, "Well, I am through gentlemen."

My uncle, Cecil Plott, was a hunting partner of Mark Cathey's. Mark's nephew, Britt McCracken, was also my uncle's best friend. Uncle Cecil shared this poignant story with me about his beloved friend, Mark Cathey: Two months after the meeting with the preacher, on a crisp October day, Mark Cathey leashed up his Plott hounds, grabbed his rifle and left home on his final hunt. His sisters became alarmed when he had not returned by dark and sent a search party out to find him.

At midnight, they found Cathey, lying at the base of a big hickory tree, his rifle across his lap and his loyal Plott dogs still by his side, guarding him to the end. Cathey's sisters had to be called to the scene to call the fierce dogs off before his corpse could be removed. He had died of an apparent heart attack.

Mark Cathey is buried in Bryson City, North Carolina, on Schoolhouse Hill, not far from other Hazel Creek legends such as Gola Ferguson, Jack Coburn, Granville Calhoun and Horace Kephart. The epitaph on his tombstone eloquently reads:

Beloved Hunter and Fisherman
Caught Himself by the Gospel Hook
Just Before His Season Ended for Good

It is a fitting tribute to the legendary guide and Plott dog man, as well as to the end of a magnificent era of hunting with Plott hounds and hunting clubs in the Great Smoky Mountains region, most notably the GSMNP and the Hazel Creek Watershed. There are few, if any, more important places in Plott breed history.

CHAPTER 6

JACK EDWARDS

"The Pick of the Litter"

By any standard of measurement, James Jackson Edwards has led a long and exceptional life. A decorated United States Army combat veteran of World War II, Jack Edwards later earned his college degree at Auburn University before eventually becoming a renowned attorney. During the Korean War, Jack put his law degree to good use serving as judge advocate general officer in the army reserves while stationed in South Korea.

At the conclusion of the Korean conflict, Edwards returned home and resumed his legal career while serving as legal counsel for several high-profile insurance firms across the southern United States. Jack's personal life was equally as charmed as his professional career. He and his beloved wife, Janet, raised two very successful children, Carol and Jim. A third son, David, died tragically at a young age from cystic fibrosis. The couple remained happily married until Janet's death in 2010.

Today, at the age of ninety-one, Jack lives alone and enjoys his retirement in Charlotte, North Carolina. He smiles as he remembers how none of this would have happened were it not for John A. Plott and his second wife—the former Nora Edwards—choosing Jack as their adopted son.

Early Years

Born in Alabama in 1926, the first five years of Jack's life seemed almost cursed. His father, Jethro Edwards, was born in Haywood County, North

Carolina, and was the brother of Nora Edwards Plott, the second wife of John Amos Plott. Jethro moved to Alabama to find work in the early 1920s and started a family of his own there.

Jethro Edwards and his first wife had three sons, with Jack being the oldest. Shortly after Jack turned four, a series of disasters sent the Edwards clan reeling. The stock market crash of 1929 plummeted the United States into the economic turmoil of the Great Depression. These tragic events left the Edwards family, and most of America, poverty stricken. To make matters worse, Jack's mother died unexpectedly in 1930, and not long after that, Jack's father, Jethro, lost his arm in a logging accident.

Jethro Edwards suddenly found himself disabled, unemployed and the widowed father of three young, hungry boys. He could not take care of them all and turned to his sister, Nora Plott, for help.

Edwards deposited all three of his sons in the living room of John Plott's home in Plott Valley in early 1931 and asked John and Nora to choose the child they were willing to adopt. It proved to be a fortuitous change of luck for Jack Edwards, as John and Nora selected him as their adopted son. Jethro returned to Alabama with Jack's brothers, leaving young Jackie Edwards as the pick of the litter for John and Nora Plott to raise.

This informal adoption by John Plott would be equally beneficial to Plott breed historians in providing us with Jack's firsthand insight on various aspects of little-known Plott family and Plott breed history. To better appreciate the significance of this, one must first realize the integral roles that John A. Plott and his son, George Ellis Plott, both played in the annals of Plott breed history, as well as the remarkable series of events that took place during the three decades between 1930 and 1960.

John A. Plott, oldest son of Mont Plott, along with his youngest brother, H.V. "Von" Plott, are generally recognized by breed historians as being two of the five most instrumental people in breed history. Thus, the Plott brothers, along with breed icons Gola Ferguson, Isaiah Kidd and Taylor Crockett, are commonly referred to as the "Big Five." They played integral roles in developing the Plott hound breed, getting it formally registered with the UKC in 1946 and perpetuating that great legacy deep into the twentieth century.

Most breed historians are quick to add that Captain George Ellis Plott—better known as Little George—the only son of John Plott, would have joined their ranks had he not been killed in action while serving in World War II. I wrote an in-depth profile of Captain Plott's remarkable life and heroic death in my third book, *Legendary Hunters of the Southern Highlands*.

Many breed enthusiasts—including Captain Plott's father, John, and his uncle, Von—differed in their approaches regarding how to best promote the breed and constantly bickered over everything from the origins of the dog to the correct breed standards and breeding techniques.

World War II hero Captain George E. Plott, better known as Little George. Captain Plott was killed in action on December 24, 1944.

But Little George Plott always rose above the pettiness and held the high ground. He was well known as a man whose integrity was beyond reproach and as an individual who could bridge the gaps within his own family, as well as among the many outside members of the Plott dog world. People with that level of integrity combined with those political skill sets, along with the ability to consistently adhere to them, are exceedingly rare in the dog business—or any business, for that matter.

As great as the Plott hound is today, it would have undoubtedly been even better had George Ellis Plott survived the war and lived a normal lifespan. His death was a loss to the Plott world like no other. We all know that now, but young Jack Edwards was among the first to recognize the qualities of the man who would become his adopted big brother: Little George Plott. And Edwards's unique perspective as a family insider allowed him to witness firsthand what many call the "golden age of the Plott breed." The twenty-eight-year span between the time Jack Edwards first arrived in Plott Valley in 1931 and the death of John Plott in 1959 was an era like no other in Plott hound history.

Little George Plott became a legendary Plott dog breeder and hunting guide during this period before dying a war hero in 1944. Scores of famous bear hunts took place across the southern mountains and across the country during this era, including the iconic 1935 Branch Rickey hunt. Hundreds of legendary Plott hounds were bred and hunted by John Plott, Von Plott and their many associates during these three decades.

Men like Hack Smithdeal and L.M. Patton, among others from across the nation, flocked to Plott Valley to get Plott hounds of their own. The breed gained worldwide notoriety when it was officially recognized as a purebred dog by the UKC in 1946 and by the National Plott Association in the 1950s. And Jack Edwards witnessed it all.

Of course, young Jack Edwards knew none of that in 1931. That was all in his future. Right then, he was essentially an orphan child, still grieving the loss of his mother, separated for the first time from his father and brothers and thrust into a strange home with people he had never met. Simply put, the child was terrified.

But as scared as he was, the lad was already smart enough to recognize that he had landed in a fine place. Journalist John Maloney described Plott Valley this way: "It is a delight to the eye, with flocks of Canadian geese, beautiful horses, fat pigs, friendly sheep, raucous guineas, sleek milk cattle, strutting turkeys and cackling hens living in amicable harmony in an orchard fringed meadow watered by a well-stocked trout stream, permeated with a bedlam of barks from the family Plott hounds."

There was plenty to eat, a roof over his head and a warm feather bed of his own, covered by thick bear hides and sheep skins. Jackie Edwards couldn't ask for more than that. He didn't think it could get any better, but it did.

Nora was John Plott's second wife. He and his deceased first wife, Harriett, had two children, Grace and George. Grace, the oldest child, was born in 1907 and was already enjoying a successful career as an administrator working in New York City and Washington, D.C., by the time Jack arrived in 1931.

Little George was barely eighteen years old then yet already a highly regarded farmer, horse and dog breeder and hunting guide. If all that wasn't impressive enough, Little George was also a deputy forest warden, and in October 1930, he carried on the Plott family military tradition by joining the local National Guard unit.

Jack was more than a little intimidated by his newly adopted big brother, but Little George welcomed the boy with open arms, immediately

Jack Edwards and Maj, 1932. *Courtesy of Jack Edwards.*

taking him under his wing. Jack recalled that he knew he was finally accepted when George allowed him to play with his favorite non-Plott dog, a mixed-breed sheep dog called Major, or Maj for short.

Maj was the only non-Plott dog living on the farm then, and Jack remembered Maj as being a great herding animal, so highly respected that the animal was permitted to live on the front porch and eat off George's plate. Jack's eyes glistened with tears as he recounted how devastated Little George was when Maj died, as well as how the next twelve years were some of the best days of his long life.

A NEW LIFE ON PLOTT CREEK

Even during the depths of the Great Depression, life on Plott Creek was good for young Jack Edwards. He offered incredible insight of a bucolic existence in Plott Valley and the surrounding region, as well as rare snapshots of fun with Little George Plott. It was an enjoyable time, but one filled with hard work.

Little George taught him how to be a top farm hand, horseman, herder and dog handler. Jack said that the family always had a least twenty head of cattle and thirty or more sheep, along with several draft horses and mules. But Jack added that Little George's most prized possessions were his beloved Plott dogs and a Kentucky racehorse.

Edwards said the Plott dogs always took priority, and he recalled them as being magnificent animals rewarded with special care and housing worthy of their preferred status:

> *We always had at least eight and sometimes as many as twelve Plott hounds on the farm. With the exception of old Lep* [Plott's Lep], *they all were almost identical in appearance—strong, athletic dogs with a good nose, almost all with beautiful brindle coats. I know Uncle John liked old Lep—he was a spotted dog—but he was the only one I ever saw on the farm that looked like that. Little George didn't like them, and neither did Von. For some reason, Uncle John did at first but later changed his opinion on the dogs, preferring the more traditional brindle Plotts instead. And we had an occasional buckskin dog, too—nothing wrong with that. All of the dogs were wary of strangers and quick to bite if they didn't know you. They were bad to fight other dogs while hunting,*

A 1938 photo of Plott hounds owned by John and Little George Plott on John Plott farm.

> *too. They were very aggressive towards outsiders and other hounds but fiercely loyal and gentle to us, and they were incredibly intelligent.*

Jack enjoyed remembering and talking about their all-time favorite Plott dogs:

> *Everyone knows about Plott's Lep. When Uncle John came back from Kansas in the 1920s, he didn't like it that Von had taken over the dogs from their father, Mont. He thought he could do it better. There was quite a bit of jealousy between the two of them. John got some dogs from Mont and found some of the old Lep bloodlines while he was working for a Civilian Conservation Corps over near Brevard in the '30s—Little George and me ran the farm for him while he was gone. I think a man named Owens had the Lep dogs over there. Anyway, John brought some back home and bred them—that's where Plott's Lep came from.*

Jack paused to think a bit before continuing:

> *You always hear Lep was Uncle John's favorite, but Beauty and Cricket were the two that he really liked most—and Beauty was my favorite, too.*

I hunted with her several times, and she was outstanding. There's a picture of me as a little boy in front of the old cabin with a pack of Plotts that everyone thought was Little George. The light-colored sheep dog in the front is old Maj, and Cricket and Beauty are in that picture with me, too. Beauty is also the dog pictured with John and Nora in front of their house, and that's her dog house directly behind Aunt Nora in the same photo. Little George had a buckskin dog named Buck that he liked a lot, too, and two others named Bute and Queen—all three of them were on the Branch Rickey Hazel Creek in 1935.

When asked how the dogs were housed, Jack answered:

Three were kept on dog runs with access to the spring race near the back of the house. Three others were kept in runs on the other side of the creek, and two more—usually the favorites—were kept near the patio and had access to the creek on their runs. We didn't have to water any of those dogs, as they all had easy access to water. Two dogs, and sometimes more, were

A 1936 photo of John and Nora Plott with favorite Plott hounds Beauty and Cricket.

> *kept up on the ridge where the apple trees are. We had to haul water up to them. It was a lot of work cleaning up after them and keeping them all fed and watered.*

When young Jackie wasn't taking care of the family Plott hounds and milking cows, he had plenty of other chores to do as well. Under the tutelage of Little George, Jack was soon able to shear up to twenty-five sheep a day, and he became an expert herder. He recalled once driving a herd of cows from Plott Creek to Bethel—a community along the Pigeon River—about fourteen miles from their farm. They would leave the cattle at Bethel in the spring and bring them back to Plott Valley in the fall. One year, the Plott family lost their entire herd to a lightning strike that killed all their cattle as they huddled under an oak tree during a fierce thunderstorm.

It wasn't all hard work, though, as the boys were constantly seeking ways to have fun. George was a history buff and had quite an extensive collection of arrowheads and other Indian artifacts that he had collected on the farm. He stored the collection in a wooden cheese box, the lid of which was decorated with drawings of a racehorse, a squirrel, a pig and old Maj—all expertly rendered by Little George. Jack was constantly awed by the many talents of his new big brother.

The family source of water was a fine, bold spring near the right rear corner of the house; Jack called it the "sweetest water I have ever tasted—never had any better, before or since." The family bathed at a small waterfall on Plott Creek above their home in warm weather and carried water indoors and boiled it for baths in colder months.

Jack chuckled as he remembers how John Plott was at first reluctant to put indoor plumbing in their house, as the elder Plott felt that it "wasn't natural for humans to shit indoors where they lived." Eventually, John complied with the wishes of his wife and built a bathroom in the house in the early 1950s.

Jack Edwards herding sheep as a boy on the John Plott farm. *Courtesy of Jack Edwards.*

However, before that, the family made do with a three-seater outhouse built over the creek below their home. Like all boys, Jack and George could be mischievous and loved to play pranks. Jack says they would often wait for folks to enter the outhouse to relieve themselves and then bombard the creek below the johnnie house with big rocks, splashing those inside with ice-cold creek water. "That would really get their attention! We never got tired of doing that," Jack said.

Although Little George never married due to his military career and early death, Jack said that George was quite the ladies' man. When Jack was old enough to date, Little George offered him some courting tips, and the two sometimes double-dated in George's 1927 Willy's Whippet. The car was a source of pride for George, even though it ran erratically. John Plott scoffed at the vehicle and said that horses were much more reliable.

Like most mountain folk of that era, the Plott clan was incredibly self-sufficient. They raised their own food and cash crops and could build most anything they needed. John, Jack and George once built a barn entirely by hand—cutting the locust trees, dressing them and erecting the structure using only brute strength, a block and tackle, draft horses, an axe, an adze and a hammer. They also built a rock springhouse on the rear of their home. This was later the site of their first indoor bathroom.

"It was a great life," Jack surmised. "I couldn't have asked for a better one. Don't forget that this was during the Great Depression too—most folks were fighting just to survive; we were very fortunate—especially me. And we always had a great time running the dogs on bear hunts."

HUNTING

As soon as he was old enough, Little George taught Jack how to safely handle and shoot firearms. George was a superb marksman and an even better teacher. It wasn't long before Jackie was an equally skilled sharp shooter. The boys spent many hours target practicing with their three favorite hunting guns. These weapons included an original model 1873 .32-20 Winchester repeater; a circa 1900 twelve-gauge, H model, double-barrel Stevens shotgun; and an 1890 8mm German Mauser military rifle. All three weapons are pictured prominently in several famous family hunting photos.

John Plott favored the shotgun and used double aught slugs as his preferred load, while Little George hunted with both the Winchester and the Mauser, although Jack said that George much preferred the smaller, top-loading Mauser with its five-round clip because of its size and knock-down power. The old German army rifle was ideal for bear hunting and navigating through rough terrain and laurel thickets. Later, when Jack was older, he used the Winchester himself on several bear hunts.

Jack revealed that his family enjoyed bear hunting as well as fox hunting. According to Jack, John Plott was a renowned fox hunter and often used his Plott hounds for such. This is yet another example of the multipurpose capabilities of the Plott dog. While not surprising, it is nonetheless the first documented record that I am aware of regarding Plott dogs being utilized as fox hounds.

But it was bear hunting that the Plott clan and their legendary hounds enjoyed most, and young Jack could not wait until he was old enough to accompany the men on his first bear hunt. Jack was only ten years old at the time of the famous Branch Rickey Hazel Creek Hunt in 1935.

He grimaced as he remembered his disappointment in not being allowed to participate, although he remembered hearing all about it. Edwards did get to meet Rickey and described him as a kind and generous man who

Jack Edwards with Plott hounds and Major, in front of Henry Plott's cabin on John Plott's farm in 1934. *Courtesy of Jack Edwards.*

personally gifted the lad with a St. Louis Cardinals baseball jacket. Jack added that he kept the garment for years as one of his most prized possessions.

It was in 1937 that Jackie finally went on his first bear hunt, and it proved to be a memorable one. The Plott family were close friends and hunted often with Osley Bird Saunooke, former Marine and professional wrestler, who won his first world championship title belt that same year. Saunooke later became a popular principle chief of the Eastern Band of the Cherokee, and even today, Jack fondly refers to him as "the Chief."

Saunooke, a full-blooded Cherokee, was a giant of a man, standing six feet and six inches tall and weighing well over 300 pounds. The Chief was a man of many talents. He loved to hunt and was a skilled storyteller with a huge appetite for life:

> *The Chief could really keep you entertained. We'd hunt all day near Soco Gap and Black Camp Gap—all over the reservation—and then sit around the campfire at night eating and listening to stories. The Chief would roast potatoes, turnips and onions—all cooked together underground with a fire over it—and barbecue a slab of meat to go with it. No one ever went hungry in his camp. We always had a good time.*

Little George and Jack would walk twelve miles one way with their dogs from Plott Creek deep into the Plott Balsams and meet John Plott, Chief Saunooke and their Indian friends near Soco Gap. The boys were in incredible physical condition and thought nothing of walking that far, not to mention strenuously hunting for a few additional days in harsh terrain.

They worked as drivers with their dogs, finding the bear sign and driving, or running, the bear toward stands, where the older hunters—or standers—usually shot them. John Plott, already in his early sixties at that time, was one of these standers and killed a bear with his Stevens shotgun on this trip.

More memorable hunting trips soon followed, including several to the fabled Hazel Creek Clubhouse. Jack said that a family friend—he believes it was Ed Lambert—had a flatbed truck that was used to transport them to Hazel Creek. The truck had side boards and a wooden rear gate and was covered with a tarp. There were no dog boxes to transport the animals, just a pack of hounds riding in the back of the truck with Little George and two other hunters. Ed Lambert drove the truck and John Plott rode shotgun, with Jack sitting on his lap in the cab of the pickup. On other occasions, Jack said that they took two or more vehicles—usually a car or two—along with the truck, and sometimes the dogs rode inside the car with the hunters.

Left: A 1942 photo of Little George Plott (*on top of truck*), Big George Plott (*on left*) and an unidentified man loading dogs at Hazel Creek Clubhouse. *From the* Asheville Citizen Times.

Below: Hazel Creek guides Little George Plott (*left*) and Taylor and Kay Wilson. Note the cook in background with a kerchief on his head.

It was a long, arduous trip, taking a full day to cover a total of almost ninety miles of twisting, narrow mountain roads, most of them unpaved. The first leg of the journey was thirty-five miles to Bryson City. There the party turned right onto old NC 288, a dirt road, and continued another forty miles to the town of Proctor and then about nine more miles up rough logging roads through the small community of Medlin to the Hazel Creek Lodge.

Jack remembered the massive lodge as being comfortable but nothing fancy, with three solid meals prepared for them daily by a male employee of the club who always wore a kerchief tied around his head. (You can clearly see the cook in the background of a classic Plott dog hunting photo. He is walking behind hunting guides Little George Plott, Kay Wilson and Taylor Wilson, all pictured in the foreground, along with their great Plott hounds.) Edwards also remembered Hazel Creek manager Jim Laws and his son, Oliver Laws, well—we'll talk more about them shortly.

Little George killed one bear on this Hazel Creek hunt with his trusty Mauser, and Jack said that the hide from that bear is shown tacked on the barn behind Jack in the photo with Maj and a pack of Plotts. Jack had to stay home and work on the farm during two other famous Hazel Creek Hunts in 1935 and 1937, although he vividly remembered hearing about them. Both hunts are described in detail in my third book.

Edwards remembered a problem with local authorities after an unplanned out-of-season bear hunt in 1941. Little George had been called into active military duty at that time, and Jack was only sixteen. A bear killed several head of cattle on their farm in February of that year, and John and Jack took matters into their own hands.

Their pack of Plott hounds struck a hot trail on the nearby Winchester farm, and the dogs made quick work of the marauding bruin and treed it in no time. John Plott killed the bear with his shotgun as young Jack leashed up the dogs. News quickly spread of the kill, and John Plott was soon charged with hunting out of season.

Jack said on the day of their trial that it seemed like they were the only ones in the courtroom *not* charged with selling or making liquor. The judge that day was none other than Felix Eugene Alley, an iconic barrister born and raised in the mountains of Western North Carolina. Alley was renowned for his keen legal mind, his folksy wit and musical skills as a banjo player and ballad singer. Judge Alley sympathized with John Plott's plight and acquitted him of formal charges but charged the elder Plott five dollars for court costs.

Little George Plott came home on Christmas military leave in December 1941. Captain Plott made the most of his time home and joined several other family members on what would prove to be his last bear hunt at the Hazel Creek Lodge. Three bears were harvested on this hunting trip. Jack missed the hunt and stayed home to tend the farm but happily recalled his pleasure in seeing his adopted big brother home for the holidays and hearing of his adventures on Hazel Creek. He had no idea it would be their last visit together.

George shared some additional thoughts with Jack about his army service, feelings that would prove to be tragically ironic. He conveyed to Jack that he was very proud to be a foot solider in the United States Army. However, the young captain added that he was especially suited for army service due to his inability to swim and confided to Jack that his biggest fear in life was drowning. George and Jack laughed together as they agreed there was little danger of an infantry man drowning—yet that is exactly how Captain Plott died on Christmas Eve 1944.

Character Insights, Breed History and Family Lore

Edwards related that Little George was stationed all over the country training troops for overseas deployment between 1941 and 1944. Jack witnessed Little George's skills as a teacher firsthand and believes that his adopted brother literally saved the lives of thousands of soldiers while serving as a training officer during this time, before finally being deployed for combat himself in 1944.

Jack offered the following insights on the character of Captain Plott, as well as several other notable characters and incidents in Plott hound history:

> *Little George Plott was the finest man I ever knew—bar none. He was always there for me in thick and thin. He taught me so many important things, but most of all, he taught me the importance of honesty, of defending your family, friends and country and always doing the right thing.*

Jack stopped a second and pointed emphatically before continuing:

> *Let me tell you what kind of man he was. When I was about thirteen or fourteen in 1938, a boy much older than me attacked me while I walked home alone from church. Even though he was older and bigger, he didn't have the guts to fight me fair and square. Instead, he hid in the bushes and*

attacked me from behind, hitting me with rocks. I was cut up badly and crawled home. I told Little George what happened and who the other boy was. He was livid!

The tears began to flow before Jack regained his composure:

After they bandaged me up, George and I went to visit the culprit. George knocked on the door, and the boy's father came out on the porch. George explained to the man what happened and that he was there to make things right. The father was a big, burly man, older than George, but that didn't matter. George gave him two choices: He could either take a whipping from George himself, or he could bring his son out to face the music. The big man hesitated as he thought things over and finally called his son outside. The boy came out—he was about the same age and maybe a little bigger than George. George told him what we were there for and then proceeded to beat the living hell out of the rascal. The father watched the whole thing and never tried to intervene. Before George finished, he made the boy apologize to me and promise never to bother me again.

Jack stared off into the distance, collecting his thoughts before he resumed:

We all know he died a hero. You wrote about it beautifully in your book. I followed his example as best I could and joined the army, too. I wanted to be just like him. I was overseas myself when he was killed, but I can tell you this: John never got over it; none of us did. The death of any soldier is tragic, and no parent expects to bury their children—it's not natural. I know, I had to bury a son of my own, and it nearly killed me—you just never get over it. But to lose someone as special as George was, so young—well, that's just a tragedy beyond words.

The words choked to a halt as Jack Edwards—a World War II hero in his own right—remembered what could have been:

What most people don't understand is that Little George could have literally done anything he wanted to with his life. The sky was the limit. There is no doubt in my mind the Plott hound would have been an even better dog had he lived, and I believe he could have raised a Kentucky Derby–winning racehorse, too. He loved Man O' War and kept pictures of the champion racehorse in his room, and he was already working on a breeding program with his own racehorse—I have a picture of it. He was the kind of man that can change the world. The kind of man you only see once in a lifetime—if then. But he crammed a lot of life into his thirty-two years, and he gladly and willingly sacrificed it all for his men and for his country. That says it all, doesn't it?

When asked his thoughts regarding brothers John and Von Plott, Edwards offered this response:

Both of them were stubborn as mules—I think that is a trait they shared with their dogs. Both were passionate about the breed, and both loved to hunt, although Von was far and away a better hunter. He and Little George would rather bear hunt than eat. George and Von could run for days. John was more refined and more educated. Von was rough, coarse; he could be loud at times, and he liked to drink a lot and tell tales. John and Little George both felt that smokers are damn fools. Both John and Von could curse like sailors, but none were better or more creative in their cursing than Von. He could cuss for an hour and never use the same word twice.

What about their dogs? Were they the same in conformity and performance?

A late 1930s photo of Jack Edwards and Plott dogs owned by John and Little George Plott. *Courtesy of Jack Edwards.*

> *That is a good question. I have heard it said that they were very different. Hack Smithdeal, who I met more than once, made that comment. But look at the photos. Other than the Lep dog, they were all about the same size and color with the same skill sets. Mostly various shades of brindle, with an occasional buckskin or black saddleback.*

When asked which Plott brother (John or Von) was more dedicated to the breed, Jack responded:

> *I once thought that John was more dedicated to doing things the right way and not as interested in selling dogs as Von was. I think there is some truth to that still, but looking back, I think a lot of their problem was jealousy. The older brother John didn't like it that baby brother Von was more famous and getting what he thought was too much credit for the dogs. And Von resented the fact that John left home and came back later to claim his own fame, while Von stayed with Mont and the family and never left the farm. Little George was the only one that could talk and relate to both of them. Had he lived, there would be none of this talk you hear today about differences in the dogs, nor would any outsider ever have been able to falsify papers or come up with their own false breed standards or their own inaccurate version of breed history. George would have stopped all that for sure.*

Speaking of history, Jack was asked about the subject of the missing eighteenth-century ship cargo manifest—the so-called Holy Grail of Plott breed history. There are two schools of thought regarding the origins of the Plott breed.

The Plott family has maintained for centuries that my great-great-great-grandfather Johannes George Plott first brought the dogs to America from Germany in about 1750. Others argue that this never happened at all, that the Plott family developed the dogs on the American frontier—thus making it an American breed with no Germanic roots.

The truth is that no one can conclusively prove it either way, and either way the end result as we know it today remains the same, as does the clear majority of breed history. Nevertheless, it seems odd that the Plott family stayed true to this version of the story for hundreds of years. Surely there must be some substance to their story, and the bulk of that substance revolves partially around the existence of the missing cargo manifest.

Legend has it that John Plott's daughter, Grace, found the document in a museum in either Philadelphia or Washington, D.C. The manifest reportedly has a specific date and ship name and lists the five Plott dogs among the cargo, describing the canines as "two yellowish or fawn colored hounds," apparently buckskins, and "three striped dogs," evidently brindle coats. Von Plott confirmed this to *Sports Afield* writer Jerome Robinson in 1973, although Plott simply referred to the original five dogs as being "three brindle colored hounds and two buckskins."

Grace Plott turned this document over to her father, who reportedly kept it in the top drawer of a chest of drawers in Little George Plott's old bedroom. A bearskin rug lay on the floor of the room and another across the bed—both taken from bruins killed by Little George.

Elizabeth Plott, daughter of Sam Plott and niece to John, slept in the room while visiting the farm with her father. She recalled seeing the document stored there but doesn't know what happened to it. Joseph Polly, a well-known second-generation Plott man from Missouri, said that another breed legend, the late Marion Todd, saw it there as well. Two other notable Plott enthusiasts—who asked to remain anonymous—said they saw it too and that Todd had a copy of it.

Breed icon C.E. "Bud" Lyon of Lake City, South Carolina, verified the existence of the document, as did Jack Edwards. John Plott himself told writer Carlos Vinson of its existence in 1946. Like all the other reputable sources mentioned, Jack's integrity is beyond reproach, and like the others, he does not know what happened to the document.

Jack said that after John Plott died in 1959, the property—including the document—was inherited by Grace Plott, and upon her passing, the entire farm and all its contents were later sold outside the Plott family. If the document ever existed, it was likely discarded as trash or else was stored away in some dusty attic, its owner clueless of its importance. It is possible that the document could also be the passenger manifest of the ship, mistakenly described as a cargo manifest. Furthermore, cargo manifests in general were not commonly used or kept on record until after 1800, so it may never have existed at all.

Nevertheless, it's hard to accept that all these reputable sources are mistaken—even more so now that we can add the credible name of Jack Edwards as a witness to that list. These sources, combined with the consistency of the ancient story itself, make it more viable than ever. But until more specific documentation can be produced, the story remains a mystery and speculative at best.

However, that path led me to yet another question regarding breed history, and Edwards offered valuable insight here, too. Jack knew Hazel Creek guide Oliver Laws well and verified that Laws and Little George were indeed friends and that both were outstanding hunters. I then told Edwards of the lengthy 1985 interview with Laws that was scheduled by

Plott breed legend Steve Fielder. Fielder was working for the UKC at that time and arranged for his friend Vance Biesecker to conduct the interview.

Vance is a fine hunter in his own right and a dedicated Walker dog man, but by his own admission, he knew little about the Plott breed. Vance wisely let Laws do most of the talking and injected questions periodically when needed to keep things moving. I have a copy of the interview and have transcribed every word of it.

Laws was an elderly man in 1985 and in poor health, though still mentally sharp. He offered a wealth of information in the interview, much of it easily documented as factual. Nevertheless, there were quite a few points that are questionable at best and several that are outright mistakes, although in fairness to him, he may have misunderstood the questions or perhaps his memory had failed him some—both of which are understandable.

However, the one item of controversy worthy of note was that Laws said Little George had told him that the Plott hound originated from Daniel Plott, son of Henry Plott in Arkansas, and that the dogs were brought *back* to North Carolina *from* Arkansas in the mid-1800s. Laws then moved on to other topics, and the interviewer never stopped him or asked him to clarify his point, nor did Laws elaborate any further on it.

Once word got out about this, many experts had a field day and embellished the story even more. Recently, it was used on a computer message board as a point of reference to disprove that the Plott family had originated the dogs in North Carolina or brought them from Germany. A prominent family genealogist added fuel to the fire when she posted a quote by a German doctor from 1837. The quote, attributed to Daniel Plott, cast some doubt on the traditional story regarding the Plott brothers bringing the dogs to America from Germany.

When Jack Edwards was told of the Laws interview, I asked the former attorney for his perspective, as he knew both Laws and Little George well and was well versed on the history of the breed:

> *That is absolutely false!…I mean no offense to Mr. Laws—perhaps his memory was failing, or perhaps he misunderstood what Little George told him. But that simply is not true. Henry Plott was the first Plott to come to Haywood County in the early 1800s, and he brought dogs with him there that he obtained from his father, Johannes George Plott, who brought them to America around 1750. Henry did have a brother named Daniel who did move to Arkansas in the early 1800s, and he came back to North Carolina to visit fairly often. He took dogs with him to Arkansas, and he may very well have brought some back to breed, too—but many people did*

> *that. Maybe that is where Mr. Laws got confused. Little George told me all that himself. He was like a brother to me; he told me everything. He never lied to me—not once. If what Laws said was true, Little George would have surely told me the same thing, but he never did. And I heard the same traditional family story from Uncle John, Von and Sam Plott too. I am sorry, but Mr. Laws is badly mistaken about that.*

Edwards hesitated for a second and continued:

> *And while we are on this subject, let me add this. I mean no disrespect to the genealogist you mention either. And like you, I agree that technology and history are both always evolving and allowing us to find new things. But does one obscure interview with little substance or detail behind it outweigh the detailed story told to me by men of honor, war heroes, veterans and kinfolk like Sam, Big George and Little George Plott? I don't think so. All the quote says is that George Plott married in Philadelphia and migrated from there to North Carolina long before the American Revolution. But that doesn't prove or disprove that he brought dogs with him from Germany, does it? Besides, even if he brought no dogs with him, the end result is the same—the Plott breed originated with the Plott family, period! Even back then, there were those trying to discredit the Plott family or take credit for their dogs. But this same story was passed down to Henry Plott, then to John, then to Mont and then to all of Mont's sons, John, Von, Sam, Big George and Robert and, of course, to John's son, Little George. Those stories were common knowledge among family members* long *before computers or most any other form of technology. I heard it from those men myself for the first time in the early 1930s. Keep in mind that the story goes back to at least the 1700s, and it has* never *changed. Yet now everyone wants to dispute it? Why is that? It isn't right and it needs to stop.*

Jack Edwards's explanation makes perfect sense to me. Yet again did Edwards fill in another important missing piece of the Plott history puzzle.

LATER YEARS

After serving his country in both World War II and Korea, Jack Edwards returned home to get on with his life. Like other members of what journalist Tom Brokaw rightly described as the "greatest generation," Edwards

Jack Edwards, home from World War II in 1946, greeted by a family Plott hound. *Courtesy of Jack Edwards.*

carved out a successful legacy of his own and today enjoys his retirement in Charlotte, North Carolina.

Jack remained in close contact with his adopted father, John Plott, until John's death in 1959. He would never go on another bear hunt or play a part in raising another Plott hound after he left Plott Creek and set out on his own.

But Jack Edwards credited the time he spent there and the people who loved him as making him the man he is today—especially his beloved adopted big brother, George Ellis Plott. Jack's insight into the golden age of Plott history makes him more than worthy of inclusion on our list of southern Appalachian breed legends. And it all began with humble origins in 1931 when John and Nora Plott made their six-year-old nephew "the pick of the litter."

CHAPTER 7

C.E. "BUD" LYON

"Beware of Bud!"

What do Atlanta criminals, black bears and car thieves have in common? They have all been chased—and usually caught—by C.E. "Bud" Lyon. We will elaborate on Bud's experience chasing crooks shortly. But regarding the pursuit of Mr. Bruin, Lyon was always ably assisted in the hunt by what most experts agree were among the world's best Plott bear hounds, and he was often accompanied by some of the most colorful and important characters in Plott breed history.

Bud Lyon is one of the few folks who can legitimately claim to have been close friends and hunting partners with Big Five breed icons Von Plott, Gola Ferguson, Isaiah Kidd and Taylor Crockett. Moreover, Lyon obtained dogs directly from these legends, and more specifically, in the case of Von Plott (and, to a lesser degree, Gola Ferguson), Bud Lyon is largely responsible for the perpetuation and correct documentation of their respective lineages.

To most Plott historians and enthusiasts—myself included—Lyon has deservedly earned legendary status of his own in the Plott hound world. That status, in many ways, meets or even exceeds these very same masters he learned directly from as a young man.

Even if Bud Lyon had never owned a Plott hound, he would have led an incredibly interesting life. An entire book could be written about his long and successful career as a soldier and law enforcement officer. However, Lyon will be the first to tell you that his lifelong dedication to the Plott breed—as well as his marriage to his devoted wife, Elsie—are two of the landmark events in his long life. "Some things are just meant to be. God blessed me with the best wife and family that I could ever have—and the best dogs too. I can't imagine my life without any of them. I have been incredibly fortunate!"

It seems somehow fitting that Lyon's journey to greatness has humble origins in the Blue Ridge Mountains of east Tennessee and that his birth and early life began near the cradle of Plott dog history, just as the breed was first gaining national notoriety.

EARLY LIFE

Chesley Emerson Lyon was born on a hardscrabble mountain farm at the head of a hollow near Bluff City, Tennessee, on July 28, 1930. He was nicknamed Bud as a baby. Bud was one of nine children born to Robert and Martha Lyon. Raising nine kids in the southern Appalachians was tough under the best of circumstances, but even more so during the Great Depression.

Nevertheless, Bud Lyon remembered his childhood fondly: "Mama took care of all us, and her job was never ending—cooking, sewing, cleaning, canning vegetables, she could do it all, and so could my father. He was a skilled stone mason, farmer and carpenter who also was a Baptist preacher. It wasn't always easy, but we never went hungry and we always had a roof over our head and clothes on our backs."

Even as a small child, Bud was enamored of dogs and hunting. He obtained his first hunting dog—a cur he named Bowser shortly before he started school. Bowser would chase most anything on four legs, and Bud said that he and Bowser once killed twenty-two squirrels in one afternoon. He laughed and added, "It's takes a lot of squirrels to feed eleven people!"

Like most mountain boys of his era, Bud roamed the ridges, hunting with Bowser from dawn to dusk whenever he wasn't working. Later, Lyon helped further supplement the family income by delivering groceries to his neighbors on what he remembered as "a big, old heavy bike, that was awfully hard to pedal." Not only did the job earn him money, but it also resulted in the youngster developing incredible physical strength. "I wasn't real big, but I had the stamina of a danged mule!"

In about 1940, Lyon had what he now considers to be a life-changing moment. A nearby neighbor had a brindle-colored female dog that had recently produced a litter of pups. Young Bud thought they were the prettiest things he had ever seen. All the youngster knew then was that these hounds were referred to only as brindle bear dogs. Regardless of their official name, the lad was impressed and determined to have some of his own.

A few months later, that determination grew to new heights when Lyon was returning home from school on his daily bus ride. He was day dreaming as he looked out the bus window, thinking about hitting the woods with Bowser as soon as he got home. Much to the boy's delight, he suddenly spied two brindle dogs racing down the road alongside the bus in hot pursuit of a fox.

"I had never seen anything like it," he remembered. "It was my neighbor's gyp with one of her pups, and they were running like the wind, giving that fox hell. He never had a chance! Neither did I. Even though I still wasn't sure exactly what they were, I knew I had to have them—I was hooked."

Lyon's interest was further piqued when he and his father made two visits to the farm and kennels of none other than the legendary Hack Smithdeal in about 1944. Smithdeal, a local prominent businessman who lived in nearby Johnson City, Tennessee, had just purchased his first Plott dogs from John, Von and Little George Plott in 1943 and would further supplement his pack with subsequent dogs from Plott family members in coming years.

Bud's father had been contracted by Smithdeal to do some stone work for him, and the youngster accompanied his dad to the job site. Smithdeal

Hack Smithdeal (*left*) and Von Plott (*right*), hunting in Michigan in 1946.

explained to the teenager the name of the hounds and their history. The cornerstone for the remainder of Lyon's life was laid that day: "Seeing Hack's dogs was the thrill of my life, and even though I was only 13 or 14, it was yet another one of those life changing moments that you never forget. I knew right then exactly what a real bear dog was, what it looked like and what it was called—a Plott hound. I had to get one, and the sooner the better."

The stage appeared to be set for Bud Lyon to enter the Plott dog world. A happy childhood filled with hard work and even harder hunting done while chasing Bowser through the hills of east Tennessee had developed him into a strong and sturdy young man. But Plott dogs weren't free, and jobs were not easy to find for mountain kids in 1947.

Lyon had to consider other career options before he pursued his ultimate objective of starting his own Plott pack. Just as soon as he graduated from high school, Bud Lyon made a visit to the nearest local recruiter and became a proud member of the United States Army.

MILITARY AND LAW ENFORCEMENT CAREER

It seemed only natural for Bud Lyon to join the military, as two of his brothers had already served valiantly in World War II and still another sibling would eventually join Lyon in the Korean conflict as well.

Basic training and military life suited young Lyon perfectly. The physical requirements—which other recruits found difficult proved to be easy for Bud. He fondly recalled running far ahead of his platoon, in full uniform, backpack and gear, leading the way on a twenty-mile hike. "I jogged the entire way and wasn't even out of breath. The Captain stopped and told me that I made it look easy and asked where I was from. The officer laughed after I answered. He said, 'I should have known that you were one of those tough Tennessee hillbillies! Only mountain boys can run like that!'"

Lyon excelled in the army and soon was promoted to staff sergeant. He was stationed in several locations across the United States before being deployed to South Korea in early July 1950. The Korean War began on June 25, 1950, and got off to a rough start for U.S. forces at the Battle of Pusan. Shortly after his arrival, Lyon was assigned to reinforce the legendary Seventh Cavalry on the front lines.

Lyon grimaced as he recalled his concern at receiving the orders. "My commanding officer said, 'I hate to do it to you, son, but you are headed to the front.' I figured that was what I was trained for, so fighting wasn't an issue. But I have to admit I wasn't happy about being assigned to the same outfit that the Indians had massacred Custer at the Little Big Horn. I didn't like that reputation much, but I had to follow orders."

Bud arrived at the battle front on July 25, 1950. It was 5:00 p.m. when an officer said, "Congratulations, soldier, you have now been promoted to machine gunnery sergeant. You are now in charge of this machine gun nest. Start killing the enemy."

The young soldier followed his orders and opened fire while he and his men steadily fed belts of ammo into their .50-caliber machine guns. Lyon recalled the fighting as being hot and heavy, with more than 1,600 Communists killed during the next two hours. Bud's action ended abruptly at 7:00 p.m. that same day when he was shot in the left leg. It would be the first of two bullet wounds that Lyon received in the Korean War.

After receiving medical treatment, Lyon returned to action in October 1950. U.S. troops had advanced deep into North Korea and were met by heavy resistance from North Korean forces, who were further reinforced by hordes of Red Chinese soldiers. General Walton Walker was the commander of the United States Eighth Army and ordered an evasive action retreat to South Korea. Lyon remembered it like this:

> *The General wanted us to move over 300,000 men in less than thirty days, down a single-lane dirt road, through Pyongyang and back to South Korea. If all that wasn't bad enough, winter was coming on hard, and we had to fight on the move. It was so damn cold that you wished someone would shoot you. It never got above zero during the day, and at night, it was fifty below zero at times, with high winds and snow. It was miserable.*

However, even in the worst of times, Lyon could find some humor in things:

> *I guess the best thing about it was that I was trained in explosives, and I really got good handling C-4. When we finally got back to Pyongyang, we had to blow up an entire supply dump that had supplied over a quarter of a million of our troops. The dump was the size of a small town, and we had to destroy it completely before evacuating the city….You can't even imagine the sight and sound of explosions like that. Now,* that *was a hell of a lot of fun. I liked blowing stuff up!*

Sergeant Lyon and his men finally made it back to South Korea at the 38th Parallel in early December 1950. He remained in South Korea until September 1951, although the war did not end until 1953. After leaving Korea, Lyon was stationed at several locations in the United States and Germany until he received his honorable discharge at Fort Benning, Georgia, in May 1954.

While stationed in Georgia, Lyon met and married his first wife, and the couple began a family together. In the fall of 1954, Lyon began an illustrious career in law enforcement when he joined the Atlanta Police Department as a patrolman.

Lyon remembered it as satisfying yet frustrating work. The infrastructure—like the military—was to his liking, and he enjoyed helping the public. But Atlanta was a big city filled with criminal elements. The Dixie Mafia was always a problem, and crime in general was high, as the nation was still recovering from the war and the Depression era. To further complicate matters, the department had just been integrated for the first time in 1948, and racial tensions were high—both on the street and within the department.

Nevertheless, despite the many challenges, Lyon excelled in law enforcement. A modest man who doesn't like to brag, Lyon reluctantly admitted that he was promoted to detective in record time. Normally it took an officer four to five years to achieve detective status, but Bud Lyon did it in less than two years.

Bud quietly elaborated on life as a big-city cop with a hard look in his eyes and jaw muscles clenched:

> *I don't like talking much about this stuff. You see some bad things working as a big city policeman. I spent two years in uniform and a little more than nine as a detective—eleven years total with the APD. But I am proud to say that I almost always got my man. Like a good Plott dog, I was determined. I would strike a trail and stay on it until I caught them. And when I did catch them, well, they could come along peacefully—or not. Either way was fine with me, and either way they were going to jail.*

Lyon left the Atlanta Police Department in 1965 to take a job as a lead investigator with the National Automobile Theft Bureau. He enjoyed incredible success in this job as well and worked for the company apprehending stolen cars and car thieves across the nation until his retirement in 1990. Before retiring, Lyon received national recognition in 1981 for breaking up a huge car ring in Chattanooga, Tennessee, where more than five hundred stolen cars were recovered and scores of thieves arrested.

However, we are getting ahead of our story. Bud clearly had his priorities in order. Once he was home from the service and employed as a policeman in 1954, the young Korean War veteran was ready to achieve his dream of starting his own Plott hound pack.

REALIZING A DREAM

Gainfully employed, with a wife and family of his own, Bud Lyon was ready to complete this perfect scenario by adding some Plott hounds to the picture. There were few, if any, Plott dogs in or around Atlanta in the mid- to late 1950s, but Lyon remained determined to find them.

In 1955, Lyon traveled to Trade Days in Scottsdale, Alabama, in search of Plott hounds. He found none there but left instead with two black and tan canines, which he later sold, as they did not meet his expectations. In 1956, a retired Atlanta detective by the name of Joe Head gave Bud his first Plott hound. It was an unregistered grade dog, but it was a good place to start.

Later that same year, Bud obtained his first registered Plott hound from Floyd Pack, who was a friend of breed icon Dale Brandenberger. She was a female named Bonnie, out of one of Hack Smithdeal's best dogs. Bud remembered Bonnie as "a damn good trail dog, but she wouldn't tree a lick." Bud later sold Bonnie and drove to Cleveland, Georgia, where a man named E.E. Kirby was rumored to have some fine Plott hounds.

It turned out that the rumors were true. Kirby had purebred Plott hounds that came directly from Gola Ferguson and Von Plott. Bud knew he had hit the jackpot here, not only with the dogs but also in first learning about breed legends Gola Ferguson and Von Plott through Kirby. Bud immediately purchased a purebred Ferguson Plott and a purebred Von Plott dog from Kirby, and the race was on!

Bud said, "It was then that I truly got interested in Plott hounds, and I mean *real* interested. Nothing was going to stop me then." However, fate took a bad turn, as the Ferguson dog was stolen and Bud had to sale the Von dog because it was a "cat killer." "Dang rascal killed six neighborhood cats in one week," Lyon quipped. "I couldn't put up with that."

A man with less determination would likely have given up the dream right then and there, but not Bud Lyon. He decided to cut out all the middle men and go directly to the primary source, and there were no better sources alive than Gola Ferguson or Von Plott in late 1956. Lyon remembered his first meetings with the breed icons:

> *I just drove up to Gola's house one weekend, and we instantly became friends. He was as nice a man as I ever met, funny and a great story-teller. And boy, did he know Plott dogs! He forgot more than most folks will ever know about them. He told me where Von Plott lived, and I met Von about two years later in 1958—we hit it off quickly, too. I loved both of them, and they were both awfully good to me.*

Bud remained close friends with Ferguson until Gola's death in 1962, and he obtained numerous Ferguson bred Plott hounds between 1956 and 1962:

> *My first registered Ferguson Plott was a fantastic dog we called Lad—his registered name was Ferguson's Lad. I hunted him several times with the great Taylor Crockett. Mr. Crockett knew bear dogs, and he said Lad was one of the best he had ever seen. He begged me to sale him that dog, but I couldn't do it. I got several more great dogs from Gola over the next few years, including two that were killed by bears. After Gola died, Mrs. Ferguson made sure that I had two of his best dogs—Mark and Bell—and Hub Plott got the rest of his pack, as Gola and Hub were best friends.*

By the time of Ferguson's death, Lyon had become a very close friend and protégé of Von Plott's. "That old man could do no wrong in my book," Lyon said. "We were best friends and hunting buddies for life. I would do anything for him." It would prove to be a most fortunate friendship for both men—one that would permanently affect Plott breed history for the better.

Not only did Bud Lyon become a beloved hunting partner and friend to Von Plott, but Lyon is also, in large part, responsible for much of the remaining early breed history that we have access to today. Just as importantly, Lyon made sure that all of Von's dogs were properly registered and their pedigrees correctly recorded, not only for establishing his own stellar breeding program but also to perpetuate the legacy of the Plott family. Von had rightfully become disgruntled with the kennel clubs and National Plott Hound Association (NPHA) by the early 1960s and cared nothing for registering his dogs with them. That is where Bud Lyon came in and literally saved the day.

Ferguson's Mark and Belle, two of Bud Lyon's earliest Plott hounds.

As I have noted in previous profiles of Von Plott—particularly in my fourth book, *Colorful Characters of the Great Smoky Mountains*—Von, although highly intelligent, was basically illiterate and never obtained a driver's license during his long life. He depended on family members and friends to take him hunting and to register his dogs, and Von depended on Bud Lyon for these things most of all. Without Lyon's assistance and meticulous attention to detail, much of what we know today about the Plott family dogs—and, indeed, Plott history in general—would have been forever lost in the early 1960s.

However, Lyon's impact on breed history wasn't just limited to his scholarly pursuit of documenting breed history and in establishing his own renowned breeding program, although both would have been more than enough to warrant his mention here. Bud Lyon would also become one of the best bear hunters to ever live. And it would soon become apparent to anyone in the sport that if you saw Bud Lyon leading a Plott dog that it would be a damn good bear hound of pure Von Plott lineage. Lyon laughed heartily as he recalled his first bear hunt with Von Plott in 1961:

Columbia, North Carolina, is the county seat of Tyrell County, North Carolina, down on the coast, not far from the Outer Banks. It has always been a hot spot for bear hunting. I took Von and his dogs and mine down there in 1961 on a hunt. It was my first trip there. Von had been going there for years, and they treated him like a celebrity. We paid three dollars a night for a hotel room, and our dogs ran a big, old mean bear right through the middle of town at noon. You should have seen it! People were climbing phone poles and jumping on top of vehicles trying to get away from all our Plott dogs and that bear!

Left: Bud Lyon and Plott hounds.

Below: Plott's Blue Boy, a maltese Plott, said to have been Von Plott's best strike dog.

The roster of illustrious Von Plott bred Plott hounds on that hunt reads like a Plott dog Hall of Fame: Blue Boy, Happy, Kate, Rock, Clyde, Flirt and Rush, plus Lyon had a few of his own Ferguson Plotts, including Lad, as well as a couple of young dogs he had recently obtained from Von. Lyon remembered Blue Boy as perhaps the best strike dog he has ever hunted with and added that Rock "could run a track with his head up that another dog couldn't even smell."

Bud eventually obtained pups out of all these dogs, all of which can trace their lineage directly back to the first Plott hounds registered in 1946. His dream now fully achieved, Lyon was determined to perpetuate and preserve that storied legacy.

Thanks to Lyon's hard work, documentation and research, we now have access to these same pedigrees today, and we can even identify the dogs on the storied Rickey hunt of 1935. Bud had the foresight to get information like this directly from Von Plott and Taylor Crockett, as well as from Gola Ferguson, who shared with Bud the original bloodlines of his renowned dogs Boss and Tige.

Von Plott and Bud Lyon hunted the swamps around Columbia, North Carolina, annually from 1961 until shortly before Von's death in 1979. But it was in the state of Michigan where they had some of their most memorable hunts. Plott and Hack Smithdeal were instrumental in getting bear hunting legalized in Michigan. They led an experimental hunt there in 1946, and Von and his family and friends returned with their Plott hounds to the Dead Stream Swamp in Missaukee County, Michigan, for yet another hunt in 1949. This hunt sealed the deal, as bear hunting was soon legalized there.

After hearing his mentor speak highly of the hunting there, Bud Lyon secured a camp of his own in Michigan. Lyon took Von Plott and their hounds with him on several additional hunts to the Upper Peninsula region of Michigan. Their first trip was in 1970, and Lyon recalled that Von threatened to shoot a local man who had stolen his dog there. Lyon recovered the hound and talked Von out of shooting the thief. Bud later purchased his own Michigan hunting camp in 1988 and has hunted there ever since. Lyon also hunted in Wisconsin, where his dogs set a record in treeing thirteen bears in less than twenty-four hours.

The Michigan incident wasn't the last time that Bud prevented Von from shooting someone who had wronged him. In the late 1950s, a nationally known Plott breeder and former friend had bought a dog from Von and registered it under false pretenses. By the early 1960s, the dog had gone on

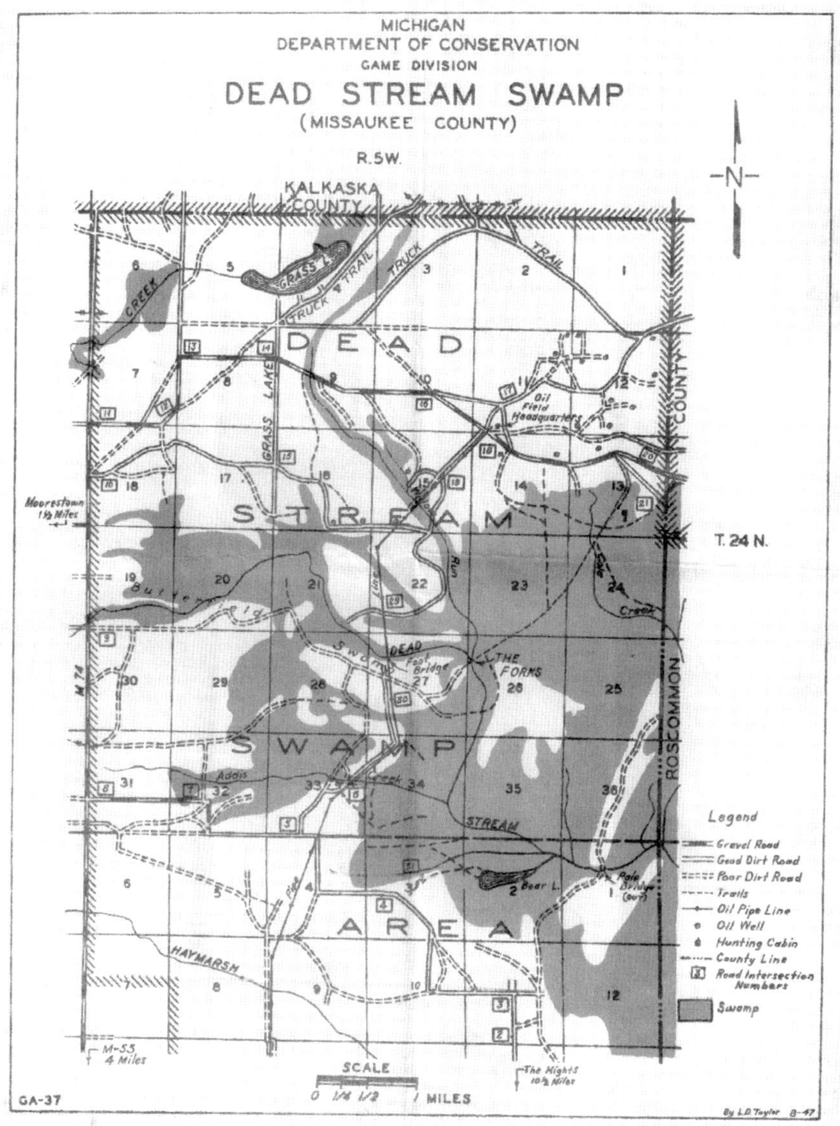

A 1947 map of Deep Stream Swamp in Michigan, site of the famous 1949 bear hunt.

to become a very prolific sire and made the breeder rich and famous. (This story is told in detail in my fourth book.)

Von was outraged at the betrayal of his former friend and vowed to kill him at the next National Plott Hound Association event held annually in the Midwest known as NPHA Plott Days. Bud can take the story from here:

Von Plott and Bud Lyon on a hunting trip.

> *I took Von to Plott Days almost every year from 1960 until 1974 or so. But that year, I think it was 1962 or 1963, he rode up with Ronnie Creasman, an incredible young hunter from Sylva, North Carolina. According to Ronnie, all Von talked about was getting his revenge on this fellow—a man we both knew well. True to his word, Von went directly to the man and threatened to kill him before Ronnie, Isaiah Kidd and me finally talked him out of it. Von meant business and he wasn't a man to trifle with—even as an older fellow. If we had not been there to intervene, there is no doubt in my mind that he would have killed that man. I am glad he didn't, but I can understand why he felt that way.*

Bud Lyon *(far left)* and Andy Blankenship *(second from left)* on a Canadian bear hunt.

For more than half a century, Lyon has hunted across the United States and Canada with renowned Plott men such as Floyd West, Rex Suddreth, Taylor Crockett, Andy Blankenship and, of course, Von Plott. But through it all, Lyon said that he has never met a man who loved bear hunting or Plott dogs more than his beloved friend and mentor Von Plott. "Von just could not get enough of it. He was the happiest man alive when he was hunting or messing with his dogs. He was one of a kind. I was very lucky to be his friend."

If all these accolades aren't impressive enough, Lyon also won numerous awards while serving in high-level leadership positions with the largest national Plott dog clubs, the NPHA and the American Plott Association (APA), for several decades. Bud's most coveted award is the Methven Big Game Award, which was presented to him by Frank Methven in 1972:

> *I have won a lot of awards in my life, but I guess that one is most special for two reasons. One, who it came from, Frank Methven. He did so much for the Plott breed and was a wonderful man to boot. Second, look at the other winners—what an honor to be included on a list with men like Gola Ferguson, Taylor Crockett, Everett Weems, Isaiah Kidd, Hack Smithdeal and all of the Plott family, especially Von. I knew all of them, hunted with most of them and considered them my friends and mentors. And look at all the other winners since then too. It's like a Plott breed history Hall of Fame. You can't be in better company than that.*

Bud Lyon has indeed successfully accomplished every dream and objective that he had set for himself in 1940 as a young boy peering out a school bus window in east Tennessee—and much, much more.

The Lion in Winter

Today, at age eighty-seven, Bud Lyon enjoys retirement with his faithful wife, Elsie, in their South Carolina home. Serious health problems have slowed him down some recently and basically ended his storied hunting career. But he remains an eloquent elder statesman for the breed, as mentally sharp and vibrant as he ever was, and always willing to offer insight and advice to anyone smart enough to listen.

Lyon's amazing connection to the Plott breed spans the better part of two centuries, more than one half of the twentieth century and still going strong more than two decades into the twenty-first. He became enamored of the Plott hound years before the breed was officially recognized in 1946, even before he knew the correct name of the hound itself.

During his illustrious career, Lyon has seen the Plott breed become officially recognized by all major kennel clubs, including the UKC, AKC and PKC, among others, and he has personally witnessed the evolution of the Plott breed from a regional phenomenon as a multipurpose southern mountain bear dog to a world-class hunting, show and service canine.

Lyon has served in leadership roles in all major national Plott hound clubs and organizations and has written scores of informative articles on a wide variety of subjects pertaining to the breed, while also serving as an unofficial breed historian. In addition, for more than six decades, Lyon was a renowned bear hunter and Plott hound breeder who consistently produced outstanding dogs, all while perpetuating the legacy of his friends and mentors Von Plott and Gola Ferguson.

Lyon achieved all these accolades by learning directly from the masters—men like Von Plott, Gola Ferguson, Taylor Crockett and Isaiah Kidd, among many others. More importantly, Lyon preserved that knowledge and passed it on to others. That alone is priceless to Plott enthusiasts.

Bud Lyon knows Plott history and played an integral role in it—he *is* Plott history. Today, as an eloquent elder statesman of the breed, it seems appropriate that we conclude our profile of him by allowing Lyon to elaborate on a variety of topics and challenges pertaining to the breed as we near the end of the second decade of the twenty-first century. Let's start with Lyon's take on what makes the Plott breed so special and discuss some of the best dogs he has ever owned or seen:

> *Plott dogs are rightfully known for their tenacity, grit, stamina, nose and athletic ability. They will strike a trail and stay with it. There is no quit*

in these dogs. But I think it is their intelligence that sets them apart from all others. I have seen them do remarkable things. Sonny Pardue was a fine coon hunter from West Virginia. He had a dog named Boss. Boss would hunt on his own and tree a coon, run back to the house and scratch on the door to get Sonny. After this happened a few times, Sonny would reward Boss with a baloney sandwich—but the dog wouldn't eat it right then. Boss would instead take it and put it in his bowl and would not eat it until the hunting was done. And Boss never took Sonny or anyone back to a tree where there wasn't a coon in it. Lots of people might not believe that, but I saw it myself!

When asked to name the best bear dogs he had ever seen or owned, Lyon paused a moment as he gathered his thoughts:

Well, the truth is I never saw too many bad ones or had many myself. Don't forget who I was hunting with and getting dogs from. Men like Taylor Crockett, Von Plott and Gola Ferguson didn't keep bad dogs. If they fed them, they were damn good—the best, in fact. Von's Blue Boy was probably the best strike dog I ever saw, and old Rock was something else, too. So was Von's dog Happy. Von always said that Link was his best all-time dog. All my dogs—and all the dogs you have—come directly from those dogs. You can't beat those bloodlines.

What about his personal best dog or dogs?

Bob, I had some great ones, you know that. Balsam Ace, Old Tom, Suzi, Big John, Speed, Blackie and Boss were all awesome dogs. But I would have to say Bull was my all-time best. On a 0 to 100 scale, with 100 being almost perfect, old Bull would get 100 across the board on all traits. Conformation, fight, grit, trailing ability, tree power and smarts—Bull had it all. Everything you wanted in a Plott hound, Bull had it, and then some.

He has hunted all over the United States and Canada. What about his favorite places to hunt and the most challenging locations?

Everyone thinks that their respective hunting ground is the toughest or most challenging. But I think most anywhere in the southern mountains is the most difficult. Not only do you have to deal with the mountains and streams, but laurel thickets, dog hobble and even, in some areas, old mine

Bud Lyon and pup, 2007.

shafts and things of that nature. There are not many roads in some of those places, and they are hard to access. It's tough going just to get to a bear tree and tougher still if you have to carry one out or, worse yet, a hurt dog. But probably the hardest place I ever hunted was out west in Colorado. Not because of the mountains either—they really were not as hard as the ones here. It was just the land—there was so much of it. That is some big *country! If you lost a dog out there, it might take you a month to find it.*

> *Plus you had to deal with elk, too. Those rascals are huge and mean—more dangerous to a dog than a bear or a hog in a lot of ways. I didn't like it out there much.*

On his favorite hunting spots:

> *I would have to say the swamps of eastern North Carolina, down around Columbia, where Von and I hunted annually for years. I liked the Okefeenokee Swamp, too, down in Florida and Georgia. Of course, I love my camp in Michigan most of all. We hunted there for forty years, even before I bought the camp. Canada was fun as well, but I'd say those swamp hunts were the best of all. Big bears, too, and plenty of them.*

I asked him if he wouldn't mind sharing his thoughts regarding the buckskin-colored Plott not being allowed in UKC and NPHA breed standards but approved in the APA and AKC breed standard:

> *Absolutely. It is a travesty that both the UKC and NPHA refuse to acknowledge the buckskin Plott as a legitimate color and part of their standard. And the reason all comes down to one word—*greed. *Some big-money breeders wanted it stopped because they wanted their competition eliminated. It's that simple. I was there when it happened, and I fought it. Von Plott, Mr. Kidd and Mr. Crockett all fought it too. Von, Gola Ferguson, Mr. Kidd and Mr. Crockett all had buckskins and liked them. It was good enough for them, wasn't it? Case closed.*

Lyon caught his breath before continuing:

> *The idiots responsible for it were told that by eliminating the buckskin from the breeding pool they would end up with a solid black dog and lose the brindle. Look around—that's what has happened to their dogs. But here's the funny part. In the 1990s, the very same people who stopped it wrote me and asked me to help them get it reinstated, but they wanted me to do their dirty work for them, as they refused to publicly admit they were wrong or that they wanted it changed. I told them that they were the ones that broke it and they were the ones that needed to fix it. I have the letters that prove all this too. Yet here we are in 2017, still debating this. It's just stupid and it's wrong!*

Amen to that. We moved on to more pleasant topics, like some of his fondest memories as he looked back over his long life:

> *I guess we ought to separate personal from professional. Personally, I am blessed to have had the best wife ever in my wonderful wife, Elsie. I couldn't live without her. I have also been blessed with four wonderful children, four awesome grandkids and some incredible step-children, too—all of whom I consider my own.*

What about professionally?

> *Well, of course I am proud of my military service and a long and successful career in law enforcement. But you probably want to hear more about the Plott hound stuff. I guess you could call my association with the breed personal, professional or both—take your pick. But outside of my family, those danged old dogs have been the most important thing I ever have been associated with, and it's not just the dogs, either—it's the Plott dog people, the owners, hunters and breeders.*

When asked to elaborate, Lyon responded:

> *It was really important to me to see that Von and Gola's legacy continue after their passing, and I think I accomplished that. I like to think that they would be proud of what we have done, and the fact that our legacy will continue for years to come through you, your son, Rusty Gill and others. Some of the best friends I have ever had I met through my association with the breed. Dudley Huber is a lifelong friend and hunting buddy. I met him when he was only seventeen and a college student while I was living in Athens, Georgia. Perry Chrisman, Doug Hoskins, Bill Hicks, Bob Arnold, Luther Wallace and the Herb Giese family down in Florida are all dear friends of mine.*

As Lyon continued, you could hear the emotion in his voice:

> *Von and Gola were like fathers to me, so were Mr. Crockett and Mr. Kidd. Hoke Rawlins was another good friend—Rex Suddreth and Floyd West, too. I helped Roy Stiles get some of his first Von Plott bred Plott dogs and Andy Blankenship, too. The list is just too long to include them all, but all of them are special and all of them have helped make me who I am today. I loved to go to Plott Days and Breed Days every year and see all my friends*

and their dogs. It was like a family reunion. And I don't mean to embarrass you, Bob, but it means a lot to me that someone in the Plott family like you is still raising Von's dogs, and it's even more important that you have worked so hard in documenting your family history and the history of our dogs. I think that would mean a lot to Von, too. I know it does to me. You have done us both proud.

After receiving what is one of the highest and most appreciated compliments of my life, I asked Bud if he could identify one defining moment pertaining to the performance of his storied Plott hounds:

I love Plott people, but I am damn proud of my dogs, too, and prouder still that they could compete with anyone in the bear woods or at a field trial—and I mean anyone. I was already developing a good reputation as a bear hunter and bear dog breeder in the early 1960s. But a lot of folks still claimed my dogs were one dimensional—that they were good only on bear. Hell, a lot of hunters want a dog that is *only good on bear. But I wanted mine to do it all, and they proved it once and for all when we beat Pioneer Drum in three out of four casts in a night hunt competition. Dale Brandenberger was one of the top breeders around back then, and say what you will about Pioneer Drum—he was one heck of a coon dog, one of the all-time best. Now, I don't think he was much of a bear dog, but that's just my opinion—maybe Dale never hunted him on bear, I don't know. But there weren't any better coon hounds than old Drum, and my dogs got right in there and beat him. I was awfully proud of that.*

When asked for closing comments, Lyon chuckled:

It's been a good run and it's not over yet. I just wish I could get out there and chase bear behind those great dogs with my friends one more time. I don't guess I ever will, but I am still looking forward to getting that pup from you and Rusty later this year. But if I had to do it all over again tomorrow, I wouldn't change a thing. That's a sign of a life well lived, and a man can't ask for any more than that, can he?

No, sir, a man can't ask for any more than that. It is further proof why C.E. "Bud" Lyon is, and always will be, a Plott breed legend. A man who in every way has met or exceeded the lofty expectations of his southern mountain mentors, breed icons Von Plott and Gola Ferguson. In doing so, Bud Lyon has become a Plott breed icon himself.

CHAPTER 8

FRANK T. METHVEN

"The Bard of the Breed"

The archives of Plott history are filled with incredible stories, articles and books pertaining to the breed and the people who helped make it great. Dating back to at least the early 1880s and continuing still today, many talented writers have written eloquently and expertly about these magnificent canines and the colorful mountaineers who owned them.

Scribes such as Horace Kephart, Wilbur Zeigler, Ben Grosscup, Jim Gasque, Raymond Camp, Carlos Vinson, John Mulhoney, Michael Frome and John Parris—among many others—all played integral roles in helping the Plott hound gain nationwide notoriety in the nineteenth and twentieth centuries. Some of them told their stories in their world-renowned books, such as Kephart's *Our Southern Highlanders* or Gasque's classic *Hunting and Fishing in the Great Smoky Mountains*, but more often, their tales were found in nationally distributed magazines such as *Field and Stream*, *Sports Afield*, *True*, *Full Cry* and *The Red Ranger*, along with multiple regional and national newspapers, most notably the *New York Times*.

Today, writers such as Steve Fielder, Danny Scoggins, Duane Smith and John Jackson proudly continue that tradition well into the twenty-first century. However, as great as all these writers are, they all pale in comparison to the bard of the Plott breed, Frank T. Methven.

Even the most casual of Plott dog enthusiasts is familiar with the writing of the late Frank Methven. After all, he wrote a monthly column about the Plott breed for more than half a century in *Full Cry* and *American Cooner* magazines, along with scores of free-lance articles for other national publications, while also writing books, including two volumes of poetry and a classic fact-based novel on Plott houndsmen and bear hunting in the Pacific Northwest, *The Sound of the Hills*.

Most Plott owners and hunters are also aware of the Methven Award, arguably the world's most coveted big game hunting award. It is annually bestowed on only the most elite of Plott hunters who have done the most for perpetuating the sport of big game hunting with Plott dogs.

Methven began the award in 1955 to honor his father and grandfather, and the list of esteemed winners reads like a hall of fame of Plott dog history. In 2009, concerned about the future of the award, Frank asked that the American Plott Association (APA) become the parent club for the award and requested that the author select the winner annually. I have proudly done so since 2010, and plans are in place for the perpetuation of the award after my passing.

These accomplishments alone make Frank Methven worthy of inclusion in this book. However, others might question how he can be included since he technically wasn't a native of the southern Appalachians. Nevertheless, I think that being born in Kentucky and having family ties to Daniel Boone and the Denton and Hatfield clans along with lifelong friendships with the Plott family more than qualifies him, especially when you consider his remarkable achievements and incredible life story.

THE LEGEND BEGINS

The roots of the Methven family tree can be traced back to ancient Germany and Scotland, but Frank's story begins with his birth in Covington, Kentucky, on October 10, 1920. He was the son of talented and adventurous parents who early on instilled in their son a love for hunting and the great outdoors. Just as importantly, they taught the lad to always believe in himself and follow his dreams.

When Frank was about a year old, his father, Frank M. Methven, left the family briefly to hunt and search for gold in California. Methven family photo albums show the elder Methven at a hunting camp in Arizona hunting cougars. Frank Sr. eventually returned to Kentucky, took a job with Hatfield Mining and soon after moved the family to Cincinnati, Ohio. The Hatfield family, famous for the Hatfield-McCoy feuds, were related to the Methvens—another interesting historical twist of this fascinating family.

By then, young Frank was already in love with the great outdoors, and he had fond childhood memories of frequently coon hunting with the family dogs. His Uncle John and his grandfather were also avid hunters, and Frank recalled often seeing what was then referred to as simply "brindle curs" or "brindle bear dogs" as a child.

Ironically enough, they *could* have been Plott dogs. Frank later learned that long before his birth, his Uncle John Methven and his grandfather frequently hunted bear in North Carolina with the Plott family. The Methven clan had a hunting cabin on Alarka Creek in Swain County, North Carolina, and they often rode the train there to hunt. On one of their visits to the Great Smoky Mountains in about 1908, they met Montraville Plott and his twelve-year-old son, H.V. "Von" Plott.

The Methvens joined the Plott family on a bear hunt in an area known as Rocky Glen, in what is now the Pisgah National Forest, near Black Mountain, North Carolina. Frank's Uncle John and Von Plott, who were both about twelve years old, stayed at the camp and took care of the horses while their elders hunted bear. Years later, Uncle John Methven recalled the pack of prized bear dogs owned by the Plott family in a letter to his nephew, Frank. Although he was not yet born at that time, Frank T. Methven seemed destined to play a vital role in Plott hound history.

Frank Jr. recalled happy times growing up in Ohio. The Methvens were not only skilled hunters but also highly educated patrons of the fine arts. Frank's grandfather was a talented poet, and his mother was a gifted singer and entertainer. She hosted a weekly radio show in Cincinnati and was one of the first women in local radio history to do so. Frank followed in her footsteps, and at age nineteen, he became the youngest radio talk show host on the Cincinnati airwaves. He once stated to me with a smile, "No one could actually see that I was young and stupid. I had a face that was perfect for the radio!"

But Frank also said that his family—like most of us—had their share of "black sheep" too. One of his relatives, Henry Methven, was a Depression-era member of Bonnie Parker and Clyde Barrow's midwestern outlaw gang of bank robbers. "However," Frank added with a wink, "we won't talk about that."

When World War II broke out, Frank T. Methven joined the Coast Guard and served on a convoy escort for destroyers in both the North Atlantic and Pacific theaters. He was on shore leave in San Diego in 1943 when he decided to attend an USO show.

It turned out to be one of the best decisions he ever made. Frank met a lovely entertainer there who would later become his wife. Her name was

Alice Jean "Jeannie" Denton, and for Frank Methven, it was love at first sight. They dated as often as they could when he was ashore. Shortly before the war ended, the couple was married in San Diego, California. Since this was Frank's home port for the Coast Guard, the newlyweds decided to make their home there.

In yet another twist of historical irony—one that perhaps foretold of their blissful future together—Frank learned that Jeannie was a direct descendant of the great long hunter Daniel Boone. Furthermore, she could trace her roots back to east Tennessee and Western North Carolina, where the Denton family were renowned bear hunters and close friends of the Plott family. The Dentons have kept Plott dogs in their family since the 1870s. Frank and Jean's union was indeed a match made in heaven.

A New Life on the West Coast

When the war ended, the young couple decided to stay in California and relocated from San Diego to Santa Barbara. Frank got a sales job there with the Carnation Milk Company. Although he excelled at it, Frank's passion was hunting. His new hometown was within easy driving distance of three mountain ranges—the Santa Ynez, the San Rafael and the Sierra Madre, all abundant with game, and Methven took good advantage of these opportunities. He quickly obtained hunting dogs of his own, but none really suited him.

Frank's quest to find his ideal hunting dog began in the mid-1940s. He recalled the brindle bear dogs of his youth, as well as the Plott hounds that his uncle and grandfather had raved about. By 1946, the reputation of the Plott breed was spreading rapidly across the country, and the UKC had formally recognized the Plott hound as an official dog breed. All these things factored into Methven's decision to purchase his first Plott dog. But it was a fateful meeting in 1948 with a customer on his sales route that truly sealed the deal.

Stuart Sharrett, a West Coast Plott dog legend, was then working as a manager of a meat market in Santa Barbara, California, when Frank first met him. The two men became friends, quickly recognizing the bond that all true outdoorsmen share.

Sharrett lived in the nearby Santa Ynez Mountains and regaled his new pal with stories of the fine hunting there. Methven was well aware of that already. But what he was more interested in were these amazing Plott dogs that Sharrett owned and hunted. Sharrett felt that Plott hounds were the best hunting dog there ever was. He invited Frank on a hunt to prove it.

Methven quickly learned that Sharrett was correct in his assessment. Sharrett's dogs were of Von Plott bloodlines, and they were the first registered Plotts that Frank had ever seen. Nothing could compare to these remarkable dogs. Good trailers, gritty, tenacious and loyal to a fault—these Plott hounds had it all.

Frank was bitten hard by the "Plott bug," and he vowed to get some hounds of his own. From that point forward, Frank T. Methven has been a steadfast proponent of Plott dogs, and no one has ever done it any better.

While Frank's first Plott dog came from Sharrett, he remembered also purchasing some of his initial Plotts from Dale Brandenberger's earliest stock. Later Methven obtained a sixth-generation Gola Ferguson Plott dog. Even then he was always looking to improve and refine his hunting stock.

Frank admittedly was never a serious dog breeder, but he didn't have to be. He constantly surrounded himself with some of the best hunters and dogs in Plott hound history, so he always had access to the finest of hunting canines. Moreover, Frank continually had the opportunity to test and train his dogs in optimal conditions, so he retained *only* the best dogs. Stuart Sharrett was only the first of the many great hunters and Plott dog breeders Frank Methven would eventually befriend.

Sharrett and Methven eventually extended their hunting range to the Pacific Northwest, specifically Washington State. It was there that Frank met such western Plott breed icons as Jerry Tuller, Ed Watkins and Doyle "Dee" DeMoss. Frank hunted there whenever he could get away from work. It was a hunter's dream—pristine wilderness with bountiful wildlife. Bears were abundant, and timber companies were paying a bounty for them. Frank planned to relocate there as soon as possible.

By 1955, Frank Methven was widely recognized as one of the best big game hunters and Plott dog experts on the West Coast. That same year, he combined that knowledge with his journalistic skills to launch a writing career that continued for more than half a century. Through his monthly columns in *American Cooner* and *Full Cry* magazines, the entire country learned about the Plott breed and their West Coast adventures. Plott owners from around the world corresponded with Frank (and one another) as they shared their insight for fellow students of the breed to enjoy and learn from. It was the first monthly national forum for Plott dog enthusiasts, and it was a great one.

Famous West Coast Plott hound Missouri Buddy Junior, owned by Gordon Larson in the early 1960s. Junior was sired by Stuart Sharret's Missouri Buddy.

It was also in 1955 that Frank began the Methven Big Game Award. Methven wanted to do something to honor his own hunting family, as well as the breed of dog that he loved so well. After careful consideration, he decided the best way to do this would be to award an annual big game hunting award—named in honor of his father and grandfather—to the individual who best represented the Plott breed.

The criteria for winning was simple: the winner had to be a top hunter who hunted *only* with Plott dogs but also, just as importantly, a breed ambassador who did their best to properly represent, promote and perpetuate Plott hounds. Over the next sixty-one years, the Methven Award would become the most coveted award in the big game hunting world, and it remains so today.

In the late 1950s, Frank met a young Californian named Gordon Larson. Methven introduced Larson to Stuart Sharrett, and the trio hunted often together. One of Stuart Sharrett's Plott dogs, Missouri Buddy, was one of the most famous of the earliest registered western Plotts. Larson bought his first Plott hound, Missouri Buddy Jr. (sired from Missouri Buddy), from Sharrett in 1961. Larson, too, was hooked, and he would keep Plott dogs until his death in 2008.

THE PACIFC NORTHWEST: A HUNTING PARADISE

In the early 1960s, Methven kept his promise and moved his family to Washington State. They opened up a restaurant called the Lion's Paw in Redmond, Washington, the heart of bear hunting country in the Pacific Northwest. The business not only provided a means of support for his family but also afforded Frank the opportunity to hunt as often as he wished. Frank T. Methven and his Plott dogs began hunting several days a week almost year-round.

Methven found true happiness in the Pacific Northwest. He and his wife had two sons, Tim and Mark, who grew up to be avid outdoorsmen, and the family flourished on their farm outside Redmond. Methven named his farm and his kennels Glen-Carin (which translates to Rocky Glen in Scottish) to honor his Scottish ancestry, as well as Rocky Glen, the North Carolina site where his family first hunted with Montraville and Von Plott in 1908. For the next thirty years, all Plott dogs registered by Frank carried the Glen-Carin name. Frank's son Mark still owns the Glen-Carin farm today.

As Methven put down permanent roots in Washington, he became friends with even more celebrated western Plott legends and frequently hunted with them. Homer Wright, who once worked for Von Plott, had brought Plott hounds to Washington when he first moved there from North Carolina in 1943. Homer lived only about forty-five minutes away from Frank in Darrington, Washington. Wright and his son, Mark, were probably the first to use Plott hounds hunting cougars in the Pilchuck River and Snohomish River Basins.

Ray Jones and Bud Hyatt also lived in Darrington and had unique connections to Plott history, too. Like Wright, they were both natives of the Tar Heel State. Hyatt was related to the Plott family, while Jones was kin to the Reece family of Lep dog fame. Southern Appalachian roots run deep in most of the Plott men of the Pacific Northwest.

Frank later obtained two of his all-time best dogs—Old Coke and Tawny—from Homer Wright and Ray Jones. Methven was always honest to a fault and recalled that while they were both outstanding dogs, they were *not* 100 percent purebred Plotts. He said they were mostly Plott, with the remainder a miniscule mix of Walker and bloodhound.

It was in the late 1950s when Frank first met Doyle "Dee" DeMoss, famous hunting guide and originator of the iconic Cascade Plott line. DeMoss also lived in Washington State. Methven said that Doyle was a gifted hunter who could read bear tracks as well as anyone he had ever seen. He further remembered DeMoss as being more charismatic than any man that he ever met, adding that DeMoss always had some of the finest Plott hounds in the world. His Cascade dogs, though allegedly controversial in their origins, are undoubtedly one of the finest lines in Plott history.

However, Frank stated that he and DeMoss "just didn't click as friends." They hunted often together and shared a passion for Plotts, but outside of that, Methven believed that they simply did not have much else in common.

That was not the case with other western Plott icons like Jerry Tuller, Ed Watkins, Gene Young, Ray Fain, Glen Buchanan, Ralph Hauck, Leo Bruce and Frank Staab, as well as the previously mentioned Ray Jones, Bud Hyatt and Homer Wright. Frank considered them all to be dear friends. Methven said that he would be hard pressed to name the best of this legendary group, but he added that if forced to do so, it would be Jerry Tuller.

Tuller's career as a hunting guide was tragically cut short due to blindness. But the western nimrod remained an inspiration to his friends nonetheless. Methven's eyes lit up as the stories flowed about his hunting partners and their great Plott dogs. Frank felt that if Ed "Pure Hate" Watkins had lived longer, he would have perhaps surpassed Tuller, or anyone else in the far west, as a hunter. Ed was a steelworker when he wasn't hunting, and he got his nickname from a supervisor who described Watkins as being "six foot

A 1960s photo of Ray Jones, Frank Methven and Doyle DeMoss, western Plott breed legends.

Ed "Pure Hate" Watkins and Buckaroo.

and three inches of muscle and brawn and 190 pounds of pure hate." Frank said that Ed wasn't a bad guy, but he loved to fight and wouldn't back down from anyone or anything. Once while his Plott dogs had a bear bayed, Ed waded into the fray and killed the bruin with a knife.

Watkins lived life in the fast lane. Frank frequently picked up Ed early in the morning to go hunting. He recalled with a chuckle that Ed was often "hung over, haggard and horny from a long night of partying." But none of that stopped Watkins from becoming a legend in his own right. Watkins unfortunately died at age forty-seven from lung damage incurred from his work in the steel industry.

During the 1960s, '70s and '80s, Frank Methven hunted his Plott hounds almost constantly in the Pacific Northwest. He traveled regularly to Idaho and hunted with Pete Ellsworth, Ray Torrey and George Ricks. Frank hunted farther north into Alaska as well. He lost a couple of fine dogs—Zebb and Jethro—when they were killed by wolves there.

When he wasn't hunting during those three decades, Methven continued to write his monthly magazine columns. The articles and the annual presentation of the Methven Award afforded him the opportunity to expand his Plott horizons across the country and allowed him to communicate regularly with other living legends of the Plott world.

Frank Methven was with Zebb the Black Baron here at an Alaska hunting camp. Zebb was killed by a bear in Alaska in 1979.

By phone, by mail and sometimes in person, Frank talked or corresponded weekly with a virtual "who's who" in Plott dog history—men like Von Plott, Isaiah Kidd, Herbert Plott, Everette Weems, Clyde Neader, Benny Moore, Dale Brandenberger, Clyde Bounds, Leroy Haug, Willis Butolph, Cheyenne Hill, C.E. "Bud" Lyon, Eugene Walker and John Jackson, just to name a few. From this nationwide network of elite Plott experts, Methven compiled a treasure-trove of historical information and photos as he became widely recognized as the world's foremost expert on the Plott breed.

Methven also met, befriended and sometimes hunted with stars outside the Plott world, too—celebrities like movie stars Clark Gable and Roy Rogers and world champion boxer Archie Moore. Methven undoubtedly enjoyed meeting these folks, and he surely could have used that platform for his own self-promotion. Instead, Frank always used that forum to bring more recognition to the Plott breed. In doing so, he exposed the dog to an entirely new audience—one that most likely would never have even heard of the Plott hound were it not for Frank Methven.

Frank supported his family with the restaurant and never considered himself a professional guide, although he was certainly one of the best ever. As he described it, "I hunted for fun, because I loved it. But more importantly, I did it for the dogs. There is nothing more satisfying to me than working with a dog, training it and learning from it. I loved and respected my dogs."

Legendary Dogs

Before his death, Frank graciously allowed me total access to his vast archives of information, and he made himself constantly available to pick his mind and question him. Being the humble man that he was, he seldom said anything about himself, preferring instead to focus on the exploits of others. I asked him many times how many bears he had treed or killed in his career. He would always change the subject and say, "a few." One day, I came across a small black and red leather-bound notebook. In it, I found one of the most amazing chronicles of hunting with Plott dogs that I have ever seen.

It was a logbook that Frank Methven kept of his hunting dogs from 1967 to about 1976. In it, he listed the name of the dog, the sire and the dam, the dates the dog hunted and the outcome of the hunt. He also included a brief assessment of the dog and how long it lived. He sometimes included the members of the hunting party and the specific location of the hunt.

Now, keep in mind that this log does *not* include the game Frank hunted for the twenty years prior to 1967. Nor does it include the game he killed or treed between 1976 and 1989. So, this is only a *fraction* of the big game that this western legend had seen behind his Plott dogs. In nine years alone, Frank Methven was a part of 444 bear kills—*in just nine years*! An average of almost 50 bears annually! In addition to the bruins taken, Frank and the twenty-one Plotts listed harvested 87 cougars or bobcats and 159 coons during that same time frame.

These are mind-boggling if compiled over the course of an entire lifetime hunting career, but this is a total for barely ten years in the sport. This does *not* include more than three decades of hard hunting that Frank Methven never bothered to document. After reviewing this logbook, historian John Jackson put it best when he said, "I doubt there is anyone living today, maybe ever, that can match or exceed this record."

I agree with Jackson's assessment but must add that unlike many hunters, no one would have ever known about this had I not compiled these totals. Frank certainly *never* would have totaled them, and if he had, he would never have told anyone about it. This can be stated with certainty for two reasons: one, I knew the modest nature of the man, and two, although the numbers are clearly recorded in his log book, they are *never* totaled. I had to do that for him. Frank was not compiling this information for his own glory; he was simply using these records to better evaluate his dogs.

To understand just how serious Methven was about his dogs and the sport, consider the following. Only one of the twenty-one Plott hounds listed lived more than four years. Most were killed while hunting, although a few were apparently stolen. At least three of them were culled, or returned to their original owner for poor performance, and those dogs were in on more than *sixty* bear kills. Frank Methven clearly had some pretty strict standards. He hunted with only the best of the best Plott canines.

When asked to list his three all-time best hounds, the old master had to think a moment. Finally, he said that Tawny was his best dog, followed closely by Cinder and Battle Cry. But after reflecting a bit, Frank added that he was reluctant to rate one above the other, as they all had unique yet similar attributes. So, we agreed to just leave it that those were his top three Plott hounds. Methven then elaborated briefly on each of them.

He got Tawny from Ray Jones in about 1958. It was one of his first dogs that originated in the Pacific Northwest. Although Frank did not keep official records then, Tawny was so special that he *did* keep a tally of her hunting totals. This remarkable female was in on more than 250 bear kills before being killed by a bear at age ten.

Frank obtained Cinder from Clyde Neader, the first of several Plott dogs—including a Lep and a few buckskins—that Methven received from the big Missourian. Cinder was his finest bay dog ever and was one of the ten Plott hounds that Doyle DeMoss took to Japan with him in 1960. While there, his party killed ten man-eating bears, and they were hailed as heroes by the Japanese people. Cinder was killed on the same hunt that Tawny was lost on.

Battle Cry was given to Methven in 1970 by probably the most revered figure in Plott hound history, Von Plott. Bud Lyon, a close friend and hunting partner of Von's, went to Plott Valley, picked the pup up from Von and shipped him directly to Frank.

Methven was extremely moved by this kind gesture. Battle Cry was Frank's all-time best strike dog, and he was in on 107 bear kills before being lost on a bear hunt at the age of three. Frank remembered Battle Cry as "a classic strike dog and a long staying dog." When Von Plott died in 1979, Frank wrote this moving eulogy both to Von and his beloved dog Battle Cry. It reads in part like this:

> *Plott's Battle Cry is now with you, Mr. Von Plott, for you are the man responsible for his creation. Battle Cry was an outstanding dog, he was hunted with men and their dogs from over half the United States and several foreign countries. He was a proud dog; his sole dedication was to that of hunting bear. Battle Cry is now with you, Mr. Plott, as he was as a puppy. He will remember your voice. Speak to him of soft warm*

Left: Frank Methven and Tawny.

Below: Frank Methven's Battle Cry, given to him by Von Plott and Bud Lyon.

days and fresh clean streams, of clear blue skies and honest men's laughter. Talk to him of towering mountains, of winding rivers, of Plott voices that sound through the shadows of the night, and of the remembered winds of a legendary day. That was his heritage and the spirit of his heart. You gave Battle Cry to the bear dog hunting world, and he now returns to you after a brief life of achievement. I miss him, Mr. Plott, but I know you are pleased to have him and all the others there with you. He bore your name proudly, and your knowing hand now rests upon his worthy head.

When asked what were the most important lessons that he could pass on to the next generations of Plott hound hunters, Methven had an eloquent response:

Breed to the best to get the best, and never breed a dog until it has proven itself first in the woods. And don't ever forget this: without a good dog you are nothing. I have never seen a hunter yet that can strike or tree a bear by himself. Dogs are everything!

THE LEGEND'S LAST DAYS

On February 11, 1988, Frank's wife, Jeannie, died with him at her bedside. It was a devastating blow to the old hunter. He retired from hunting in 1989, and shortly after that, Methven decided to distribute the remainder of his Plott pack to friends who could still hunt them. Ironically, this was about the same time that the State of Washington outlawed big game hunting with hounds.

Later, Methven waged war against several bouts of cancer and beat it back repeatedly. A lesser man experiencing all these setbacks would have given up long before that and died, but not Frank Methven. Despite his trials and tribulations, Methven continued to promote the Plott breed. In his monthly columns, as well as his books and the annual Methven Award, Frank Methven remained an inspiration and mentor to all Plott hound enthusiasts right up to the end.

Three years prior to his death, at the age of eighty-eight, Frank traveled alone across the country in March 2008 to attend APA Breed Days in Hickory Grove, South Carolina. There were no fewer than eleven former Methven Award winners there to greet him. At one point, C.E. "Bud"

Frank Methven with Sadie and Cudjo.

Left to right: Plott breed legends Frank Methven, Duane Smith and Cheyenne Hill at APA Breed Days.

Lyon, Duane Smith, Cheyenne Hill, Steve Herd, Jim Pfister, Eugene Walker, Steve Fielder, Ellet Bias and John Jackson gathered around Frank to talk. The Bard of the Breed was holding court one final time. It was a memory I will never forget.

Frank Methven's rich and full life spanned almost the entire twentieth century and more than a decade into the twenty-first. After multiple cardiovascular issues and several bouts with cancer, the old warrior's valiant heart finally gave out in late 2011 at the age of ninety-one. A fighter to the very end, Methven was still talking Plott dogs until the day he died, proudly carrying the Plott hound torch to his grave.

Upon learning of his death, 1972 Methven Award winner C.E. "Bud" Lyon said it best. "No one, and I mean no one, has done more to promote and perpetuate the Plott breed than Frank Methven. No one." Truer words were never spoken. Regardless of his place of birth, Frank Methven indeed remains the best spokesman and ambassador that the Plott breed has ever had. Because of that, and due to his close ties to the region, he will forever remain a Plott breed legend of the southern Appalachians.

CHAPTER 9

POCAHONTAS PLOTT KENNELS

"They Can Do It All!"

Many outstanding strains of Plott hounds originated in the second half of the twentieth century. The renowned Weems dogs of Everette Weems, the Swampland Plott hounds of Leroy Haug, the Gantte line of Charles Gantte, the Dixie Plotts of Robert Jones and the Bear Pen hounds of Homan Fielder are just a few that immediately come to mind.

However, when you consider the well-documented achievements of Eugene Walker and his Pocahontas Plott line, no one can deny that these dogs are at or near the top of any short list consisting of all-time great Plott hound lines. And the Walker family—particularly Eugene and Ann Walker and their son, Sam, along with Gene's brothers, Curtis, Norman and Vernon Walker—rank among the most distinguished and well-respected families in breed history.

The story of the Walker family is similar to the Plott family in that both clans have deep roots in the southern Appalachian Mountains, and they both were renowned for their superb dog breeding programs and hunting skills. Both families have also gained fame for the all-around talents and versatility of their dogs. Of course, the Plott family were the originators of the breed and have been involved with Plott hounds for more than 260 years, while the Walker family is relatively "new" to the game, as they didn't enter the Plott hound arena until the mid-1970s.

But the Walkers were quick to make up for lost time. In less than half a century, Eugene Walker has refined his Pocahontas Plott line to become some of the best Plott hounds in the world today. Moreover, his Plott line has the all-around record to back up this claim. Walker's dogs have won countless coon and big game events, as well as bench and field competitions. They are widely recognized as one of the most coveted bloodlines in the modern Plott hound world and have been for decades.

Perhaps most important is the fact that the Pocahontas Plotts are so versatile. Walker described them best:

> *People often ask me if my dogs are coon bred or big game bred Plotts? My response is simple—they are Plott bred. By that I mean they are good on small or big game—bear, cats, coons or hogs. A real Plott bred dog can do it all. They can hunt either big or small game equally well. And I consider my dogs to be Plott bred.*

Most experts would agree that the Pocahontas Plott hounds are indeed real Plott bred dogs. They are truly multipurpose hunting dogs that are well known for their tenacity and versatility, and their incredible story matches their magnificent skill sets.

Like the Plott family, the story of Eugene Walker's journey to fame comes from humble origins. Walker's father, Ed, moved to Pocahontas County, West Virginia, in the early 1900s seeking to make his fortune as a logger, teamster and farmer. He was a man as tough as the country he chose to settle. Even today, as the least populated but second-biggest county in West Virginia, Pocahontas County is a rugged mountain paradise abundant with game and well known for harsh winters.

Ed Walker and his wife, Madeline, carved out a large farm in this wilderness and together raised eleven children—seven boys and four girls. The Walkers worked hard but lived well. They grew various crops and made maple sugar and syrup, while also raising beef cattle and sheep. The farm remains in the Walker family today.

Even though much of their time was devoted to farm work, the Walker brothers always found time to hunt. Like most mountain folks, hunting was a way of life for the Walkers, as it helped feed their family. Eugene "Gene" Walker recalled hunting from the time he was eight years old and was barely big enough to carry a gun. "My love for hunting began at a young age," Walker said. "Bullets were not cheap and not to be wasted—you learned to be a good shot fast. And you had to be, as a large percentage of the meat on our table came from hunting. We were proud to bring home food to help the family out. But we enjoyed it too. We had no television in our home, and we only used the radio for weather reports and news."

Walker laughed and continued, "The mountains make you tough. You had to be to run after the dogs and the game. People pay big money for health club memberships to get in shape now. But hunting kept us in top physical condition and we didn't even know it!"

Nevertheless, Walker knew that physical fitness was only part of being a successful bear hunter. You needed good bear dogs too, and even then, young Gene Walker knew that there was nothing better than a Plott dog. He clearly remembered seeing his first Plott hound in 1955 at the age of ten. "My uncle Riffe, from Ohio, had a Plott dog. He was a Timberline bred Plott from Wayne Jeffries. My Uncle used him to hunt squirrels; he was the first registered Plott dog I had ever seen." Eugene said it was the best squirrel dogs that he had ever seen: "I knew then that I liked them, and I made my mind up to one day get me some Plotts."

However, it would be a while before Gene made good on his promise. In the meantime, he honed his bear hunting skills with some of the most renowned bear hunters in Pocahontas County, all of whom had good hunting dogs—but no Plotts.

One of Walker's foremost mentors was the late Argile Arbogast, who died a few years ago at the age of ninety-six and hunted bears until shortly before his death. Arbogast favored the black and tan breed and allowed young Gene to gain valuable experience handling his hounds. Arbogast also ran the local Western Auto store and was one of the first locals to use a CB radio. Walker quipped, "We thought that was really a big deal. The range was very limited, but what a treat!"

June Galford, who hunted well past his 100th birthday and killed a bear at the age of 99, was yet another strong influence on Walker. Galford had great success with blue ticks and redbones. Lee Dean affected Walker's career as well, as he allowed young Eugene to handle his dogs and shared his extensive knowledge with the lad.

Another local nimrod whom Walker remembered fondly was the late K.K. Wymer. Wymer was half Cherokee Indian, and Gene said that Wymer was the best tracker that he has ever seen: "Wymer could track a bear on dry ground, across rocks, better than most men could in a deep snow. He was really talented and he taught me a lot—a truly amazing person. Wymer just somehow seemed to always know the path a bear was always going to take."

Walker maintained that many of the so-called expert hunters of today could not hold a candle to these men. This was an era long before tracking collars, radios and four-wheelers. It was a time when a hunter was measured by how close he could follow his dogs on foot, and it was imperative that they did so to not lose dogs: "We didn't use a rig back then to strike a trail from a truck on the road. Back in the '60s, all hunts started on the ground. We once looked for a bear track for eighteen straight days, and I mean walking ten hours a day, every day, actually looking for sign. On the nineteenth day we finally found it, and the race was on!"

Although he did not hunt with Plott dogs then, he nonetheless ran into West Virginia Plott legends like Isaiah Kidd and Homan Fielder in the bear woods. Walker admired both of them greatly. It also made him more determined than ever to obtain some Plott hounds of his own. And by the late 1960s, he achieved that goal.

Gene obtained his first three Plott hounds in 1968. These three dogs would be the foundation stock for the Pocahontas Plott hound line. The pups—Belle, a female, along with Rattler and Lead, both males—originated from two esteemed Plott breeders, Dale Brandenberger and Kermit Allison. On the Pioneer Kennel/Brandenberger side, they descend from Pioneer Jake and Pioneer Drum. On the Bear Creek/Allison side, they come from Bear Creek Tony and Tip. Walker elaborated, "I was already obsessed with the sport of bear hunting, but it meant even more to me once I had my own registered purebred Plott dogs—I was really hooked then!"

Walker was pleased with these early Pocahontas Plott dogs. They performed well as he worked to establish his own line. Gene loved the tenacity of his first Plott dogs, and he especially appreciated their exceptionally keen cold nose. But he found that they were too big and often too slow for the steep and thickly wooded West Virginia mountains.

Walker began to study the science of dog breeding more closely. Like the old-timers before him, he bred only for results, and he would only breed a dog after it had proven itself on the game trail. He was determined to breed the best to the best, and he would accept nothing less. Walker was adamant that only the best qualities could be in a Pocahontas Plott hound.

A defining moment in his kennel history came in the late 1970s when Gene bred his Belle gyp to Gib Thompson's stud dog, Mack. Out of that cross came three of his finest Plott hounds: Hacksaw, Charlie Brown and Lucy. Hacksaw would later be the first of *eight* NPHA Hall of Fame Plott Hounds.

In 1978, big game was extremely scarce in Pocahontas County, but thankfully it has made a resurgence today. However, with so few bears left to hunt back then, Walker turned to coon hunting. Charlie Brown became his national champion coon dog that same year. Charlie Brown's 1978 record-setting three-night score of 1,700 plus points at NPHA Plott Days has never been broken. Since then, Walker has had the highest-scoring Plott hound of the year five more times with five *different* dogs.

By 1980, the Pocahontas Plotts were gaining nationwide acclaim, and Walker felt that he was heading in the right direction. But something still wasn't quite right. In his quest for a smaller, faster Plott that still retained the other desirable qualities of his early stock, Walker brought a dog named Gator into his lineage. He purchased Gator from Virginian Jack Farley in about 1980. Gator, with strong Hack Smithdeal and Gola Ferguson bloodlines, further refined the Pocahontas lineage and became a NPHA Hall of Fame winner in 1985.

Walker was satisfied with the results from introducing Gator to his line, and he stuck with it, always staying true to his lineage. Gene bred back and forth, always line breeding and never deviating from his established champions. He culled as needed and continually worked to improve and refine his already great bloodlines. The result was the refined, modern-day Pocahontas Plott. But Gene wasn't through yet, not by a long shot.

He became more actively involved in the NPHA and later the APA. Gene camped with breed icon Mack Stewart at his first NPHA Breed Days held in Boonville, Indiana. Walker fondly remembered Stewart and described him as "a very nice man. Very down to earth, just a good old country boy." Stewart had already developed his own line originating from Gola Ferguson, and Walker recalled Stewart's Bullet Dog as being one of the finest Plott hounds that he has ever seen.

By the mid-1990s, the Pocahontas Plott Kennels were well established around the world. Gene Walker had shipped his renowned dogs all over the globe and was featured in hunting magazines distributed internationally. His dogs were especially popular in Japan. If you ever get to talk to Gene, get him to tell you the story about the Japanese writer who visited with him and ate raw deer meat while it was being skinned. It is a hilarious story; I guess you can call it deer sushi?

With a consistent list of hall of fame dogs—great on both big game and coons—and with continual awards worldwide for his many personal achievements, most breeders would have chosen to rest on their laurels. But not Eugene Walker. Instead, he continued to look for ways to continually improve his bloodline.

Walker liked the grit of Lawrence Porterfield's Crockett Plott dogs. He was close friends with Porterfield and later introduced some Taylor Crockett and Isaiah Kidd bloodlines to the Pocahontas line. He was exceptionally pleased

Left: Gene Walker with Pocahontas AJ II, 1993 NPHA high-scoring dog of the year.

Below: Plott legends Taylor Crockett, Lawrence Porterfield and Gene Walker at Plott Days. *Courtesy of Gene Walker.*

with these results. Gene's Thunder dog came from Porterfield lineage, and Buffy—a dog nominated several times for the NPHA Hall of Fame—is out of Thunder. Although Buffy hasn't made it yet, more hall of fame dogs that did make it—like Gator II, Joy and Sting II—were soon to follow.

Gene remains active with the West Virginia Bear Hunters Association and has played an integral role in increasing the bear population by helping refine game laws in his native state. Bear sightings and bear hunting are common now, as the bear population is at a record high across the Appalachian range. The sport of bear hunting is more popular than ever before in the state of West Virginia.

The kill season is short in the Mountaineer State—just the month of December—and the weather is often brutal. But the results are usually good, and training is allowed year around. However, Walker strongly believes that bears should only be run from May through December to allow them time to develop and grow.

As bear hunting regained its popularity in West Virginia, Walker built a hunting camp a few miles from his home in Hillsboro. He owns seven acres there, and his land is bordered by almost 200,000 acres of privately leased and public game lands. It is a bear hunter's dream, and it has proven to be a superb proving ground for his Pocahontas Plott line. Gene keeps part of his pack there full time, training from May until gun season starts in December.

Walker starts his hunts from a rig. He was among the first ever to do so in West Virginia, and he laughed as he told me that he has literally destroyed "about a million dollars' worth of vehicles" while bear hunting, including one that he sunk while attempting to cross the Greenbrier River. Gene said that he believes in doing everything 100 percent and expects the same from his vehicles and, more importantly, his Plott hounds.

Today, at the age of seventy, Walker is partially retired from a successful career as a law enforcement officer, yet he remains a force in the Plott hound world. For almost half a century, the Pocahontas Plott line has been recognized as one of the top strains in Plott breed history.

In addition to his eight NPHA Hall of Fame dogs, five Dual Grand Champions and multiple record-setting coon hound champions, Walker has won the coveted Isaiah Kidd and Methven Awards, both awarded annually to the hunters and breeders who have contributed the most to the Plott hound breed, as well as NPHA Big Game Hunter of the Year, Timberline Handler of the Year, National Coon Hound Hall of Fame and Rare Breeder of the Year. The list goes on and on, too many to list them all here, but you get the picture.

Frank Methven presenting the Methven Award to Gene Walker at APA Breed Days.

Equally as impressive as his dogs is the reputation of the man himself. Walker is quick to credit his devoted wife, Ann, as being the pillar of his success. Ann, a registered nurse, has been Gene's soul mate for forty-five years. Her devotion to both Gene and the Plott breed has played a huge role in Walker's personal and professional success, as Ann has supported and encouraged Gene in all his endeavors. So, too, has their son, Sam, now a successful computer executive in Lewisburg, West Virginia.

Walker rightfully takes pride in his dogs but also in keeping them affordable to the common man. Although he has a lengthy waiting list for his pups, he nevertheless has not succumbed to the greed of many breeders. Walker's prices are reasonable, and stories abound of his generosity in giving pups to children. Gene has stayed true to his dogs and to his customers.

He guarantees his pups and has only had a handful returned in almost fifty years of business. Gene maintained that he has always tried to treat folks the way he likes to be treated—fair and square. And most importantly, he is emphatic that it has never been just about money with him. A great dog is the all-important end result, and it is the only thing that matters to him.

While Walker is quick to point out the strengths of his line, understandably so, he is nonetheless careful never to disparage the dogs of other breeders. He adheres to the old adage that if you can't say something good, then don't say anything at all.

Walker still is a man of strong opinions, and he will share them if asked to do so. In several recent lengthy conversations, Gene shared with me his thoughts on many Plott hound–related topics. First and foremost, I wanted to know what he attributed his breeding success to and if he would share any secrets of the trade. Gene said that there are some things that he prefers to keep to himself. But he gladly shared the following tips:

I believe the secret is in having outstanding females. I have always preferred female dogs. I have found females easier to handle, and most have a better disposition. Fifteen of the twenty-two dogs I own today are females. I believe that it takes several generations to refine a strain and get it dialed in to what you want. What you end up with depends on what you start with. Breed the best to the best, stay true to that, and you should be okay. Watch the personality of your dogs closely. There is a thin line between grit and being overly or dangerously aggressive. A dog that is too aggressive is more likely to get killed by bear or in a fight with another dog. I won't put up with that.

Walker added:

If you look at my dogs today you will find a fast, cold nosed, intelligent, easy-handling Plott with a great disposition and outstanding stamina. They have a great mouth—I think the best in the breed. My dogs aren't real big; I bred the big size out of them for this rough terrain. I only have had a couple of dogs that weighed close to seventy pounds. Most of mine are in the fifty- to fifty-five-pound range—just as they are supposed to be in the official breed standards.

He continued:

As for color, I prefer a brindle Plott. The biggest problem I see, ten years from now, is that if we aren't careful we are going to end up with a solid black Plott. You see signs of that already. And as for the buckskin, I believe that it is a legitimate color and that it should be an acceptable part of the breed standard—but only *if the breeder is honest and is willing to provide a proper DNA test. I have had some good buckskin Plotts.*

Walker paused as he carefully considered his words:

I think show dog people are hurting the breed. Breeding just for looks and show is no good—it will ruin the breed. They are another reason for the solid black dog. I also think these two-hour coon hunts, and hunting off buckets, is taking a lot of the hunt out of our dogs. There is no challenge to that, and to me, these things take away from the reputation of the old-time Plott.

When asked to name his all-time favorite dog or dogs, Walker said that would be impossible. His eight hall of fame dogs would all make the list, as would his best strike dog, Jill, which was also a night champion coon dog. And we can't forget the great Poncho and Cody II. He felt that it's really hard to narrow it down to just one.

As he reflected on his illustrious career as one of the foremost breeders of the modern-day Plott hound, Gene is proud of his accomplishments yet humble. He takes pride in the fact that his family has remained an integral part of the perpetuation of the Plott breed. And he is quick to credit the early pioneers of Plott breed history, as well as the many old-timers who took the time to mentor him as a youngster. Without them, there would be no Plott breed and indeed no Pocahontas Kennels. Walker will never forget that, and just as importantly, he has instilled that belief into future generations of Plott enthusiasts. The legend of the Pocahontas Plotts is guaranteed to endure for years to come, and what better legacy can any man leave than that?

The saying goes that there is an even greater woman behind every great man. That is certainly true with Gene Walker. Gene's wife, Ann, offered her insightful perspective of the Walker legacy:

Gene Walker with his hall of fame dog Pocahontas Cody, as well as the last bear that Cody ever treed alone. *Courtesy of Gene Walker.*

Left: Gene Walker with King Cobra II. *Courtesy of Gene Walker.*

Right: Gene Walker with Pocahontas Gus, 2003 NPHA Big Game Dog of the Year. *Courtesy of Gene Walker.*

Left to right: Gene Walker with grand champion Plott hound Pocahontas King Cobra and Sam Walker with hall of fame Plott hound Pocahontas Gator II. *Courtesy of Eugene Walker.*

> *The great highlight for the Walker family and the Pocahontas Plotts are the great friends that we have made as a result of the dogs. Some of our dearest and truest friends have been made due to our association with the Plott breed. And we definitely would not have visited many parts of this beautiful country had we not been traveling with the dogs.*

Gene agreed with his lovely wife and added:

> *I look back over the years at all the money I spent on hunting and dogs, and we could easily own a nice vacation home on the beach—bought and paid for. But without the Plott hound, I would never have met some of the nicest people in the whole world. Many of them are now my very best friends. Money can't buy that—it's priceless. I never go to a hunt or an event that I don't meet a new person with great interest in the Plott breed and in learning more about them. That always brings pleasure to me—and now, more than ever, it remains my hope that the Plott hound will be the forerunner of* all *dog breeds.*

The Walker family are classic examples of the southern mountain families *not* named Plott who helped make the Plott hound famous, and they are truly deserving of the title Plott breed legends. All Plott enthusiasts owe a debt of gratitude to Eugene Walker and other esteemed Plott owners who aren't Plott family members who have helped carry the torch of the Plott clan deep into the twenty-first century.

CHAPTER 10

YOUNG GUNS

There are scores of other Plott breed legends of the southern Appalachians whose stories deserve to be told. A few who come immediately to mind are Hoyte Dillingham, Mack Stewart, Hack Smithdeal, Charles Gantte, Hugh and Roy Clark, Ira and Gerald Jones, Eddie Hoge, Clydeth Brown, Kermit and Marion Allison, Gene White, Berry Tarleton, Rex Suddreth, Floyd West, Jerry Gosnell, Roy Stiles, Gerald Phillips, Glen Braswell, Burdet Brinkley and Wayne McCurry, among many others too numerous to mention. And just like the breed icons included in this book, none of them was, or is, related to the Plott family. Time and space prevent in-depth details about them here, but hopefully we can feature their stories in future books and/or magazine articles, as all are indeed worthy of inclusion.

However, aside from not being Plott family members and being fiercely dedicated to the breed, these individuals all share yet another common trait: they graciously shared their immense talents and knowledge with the younger generations that followed them—just as most of the individuals profiled in this book have done.

In other words, to ensure that the legacy of the Plott breed is properly perpetuated, they all have passed, or are passing, their own Plott torches for future generations to carry on. Some of these legends are gone now. But all of them, living or dead, were once "young guns" eager for knowledge, persistently seeking the advice and guidance from breed icons who preceded their own respective generations.

The 1972 Methven winner C.E. "Bud" Lyon is a perfect example of this. Lyon humbled himself to learn from breed pioneers like Von Plott and Gola Ferguson. Yet after becoming a master himself, Lyon remained modest, gladly sharing his knowledge and expertise with the world. Moreover, and perhaps more importantly, Lyon never took credit for any of it, just as he told me in 2016:

> *The reason all these people come to us for Plott dogs, or to learn about them, is* not *because of us, Bob. It's because of all the people who came before us. Folks like your family members and their friends. You and me aren't responsible for the success of their dogs—we inherited them. But we* are *responsible for carrying on their legacy. And we further honor them by doing things the right way, and by sharing their story, their history and their dogs with others.*

The 2012 Methven winner Ira Jones of Whittier, North Carolina, eloquently added, "If it's not broken, there is no need to fix it. These dogs were passed on to us. It's our responsibility not to mess it up. We just have to keep it going."

Ira's father, Gerald Jones, co-winner of the 2012 Methven Award, did exactly that. He got his first Plott dogs from Hub Plott and Tom White and stayed true to that lineage for years. Gerald, in turn, passed his knowledge and his dogs to his son, Ira, who now is passing the torch on to his own son, Clay Jones.

Thanks to that sort of Herculean commitment, the Plott hound remains the premier big game hunting dog in the world today. But with increased restrictions in hunting regulations and hunting land, there are fewer hunters, and wild game populations are at an all-time high. Hunters and Plott hounds are still needed to keep the environment balanced—or in keeping the Circle of Life complete, as the ancient Cherokees believed.

Fortunately, the members of a new generation of young guns have accepted the mantle as they eagerly carry the Plott breed torch deep into the twenty-first century. Robert Stiles of Robbinsville, North Carolina, is a classic example of this. Robert's father, master bear hunter Roy Stiles, roomed at the home of Big Five legend Gola Ferguson while he was a student at Western Carolina University.

After embarking on a successful career as an educator in Swain County, North Carolina, Roy obtained his first Plott hounds from Bud Lyon and later acquired dogs from Lawrence Plott. These dogs were the foundation stock of the close to fifty superb Plott hounds that the Stiles family and their friends still hunt with today.

Over the past four decades, 2005 Methven Award winner Roy Stiles and his storied dogs have hunted across the nation and have received worldwide acclaim. Roy's son, Robert, has hunted with his father since he could walk; now in his late twenties, Robert is widely recognized as one of the best bear hunters and Plott dog men in the southern Appalachian range.

The late, great Taylor Crockett once called Andy Blankenship of Hayesville, North Carolina, "the finest young bear hunter that I have ever seen," extremely high praise from a man of Crockett's esteemed status. Today, Andy—a 1986 Methven Award winner—still often hunts with Roy and Robert Stiles and has passed his wealth of knowledge and Plott dogs on to his own son, Andrew Blankenship Jr., yet another highly regarded young gun.

Speaking of Taylor Crockett, American Plott Association (APA) charter member, Plott historian and 2006 Methven Award winner John Jackson carries the torch for his late mentor, Taylor Crockett, by raising the Crockett Plott hounds at his Little Elk Kennels, near Boone, North Carolina. And soon Jackson will be introducing his new grandson to the world of bear hunting and Plott hounds.

No one has mentored more young guns than the self-proclaimed "old man from the mountain," eighty-five-year-old Eddie Hoge of Bland, Virginia. Hoge, the 2017 Methven Award winner, has made it his mission to introduce young folks to the sport. Every year, he participates in Virginia youth day hunts, where experienced hunters take youngsters hunting for the first time. Eddie has even gone as far as to purchase customized bumper stickers to encourage youthful participation in the sport.

Not only is Hoge one of the foremost respected elders in the Plott dog world, but he is also one of the few surviving members of Hack Smithdeal's famed "brush busters." The brush busters were mountain boys from Western North Carolina, east Tennessee and southwestern Virginia hired by Smithdeal to handle and hunt his dogs. All of them were superb woodsmen, hunters and dog handlers.

Smithdeal, a wealthy Tennessee businessman, purchased his first Plott dogs from the Plott family in the mid-1940s. For years after that, Smithdeal and his brush busters hunted them hard and often, sometimes accompanied by celebrity friends such as country music star Roy Acuff. Eddie Hoge is, quite frankly, the last of a breed, and he is truly one of a kind.

So, too, was the late Hoyte Dillingham, yet another former Methven Award winner, who was instrumental in getting the Plott hound recognized as the official state dog of North Carolina in 1989. Dillingham, of Barnardsville, North Carolina, was also renowned for his Big Ivey Plott hound line. Young guns Kevin Profit, Billy Bailey and David Williams all proudly perpetuate that legacy today. APA president David Williams, a young gun in his own right, has also mentored several younger hunters and has recently introduced his beautiful daughter, Anna Jo, to the sport.

Tennessean Roy Clark learned from the best: his late father, Hugh Clark. Roy and Hugh Clark won the 2010 Methven Award, and their Laurel Mountain Plott hounds are highly coveted across the nation. In addition to his own granddaughters, Roy Clark has mentored legions of young hunters, most notably Spanky Holt and Mike Mehaffey, to name just two.

Wayne McCurry of Burnsville, North Carolina—the 2016 Methven Award winner—has long been recognized as one of the toughest and best hunters in the southern mountains. He has raised outstanding Plott dogs for decades and is one of the world's nicest guys and best storytellers. Although he can spin a tall tale with the best of them and is blessed with a razor-sharp sense of humor, Wayne's word is gospel. If he tells you something is the truth, you can take it to the bank.

Wayne has hunted with many of the all-time greats, but he said recently that he considers his protégé, Justin "Woodrat" Gurley, also from Burnsville, to be the finest young hunter and Plott man that he has ever seen. That's strong praise from a great man and very well deserved. Justin is fortunate that Wayne and his crew graciously took him under their wing.

Thanks to these young guns and their mentors, along with many others, the Plott breed torch continues to burn brightly today. And it will undoubtedly do so for many decades to come. Furthermore, I have no doubt that these young guns will create legacies of their own, thus ensuring that there will always be Plott breed legends of the southern Appalachians for future generations to enjoy and learn from.

BIBLIOGRAPHY

In addition to the sources listed here, please read the acknowledgement section of this publication for a list of the many individuals who were interviewed for this book. It is quite an impressive list, and this book could not have been written without their invaluable input. Three of John Parris's great books are included in the following bibliography. But his newspaper columns, published several times weekly in the *Asheville Citizen Times* from the 1930s to about 1980, also provided a wealth of information. It would take several pages to list them all. Time and space prevent that, but suffice it to say they are worthy of at least brief mention.

Aiken, Gene. *Stories from the Great Smoky Mountains*. Gatlinburg, TN: Buckhorn Press, 1990.

Alley, Felix. *Random Thoughts and the Musings of a Mountaineer*. N.p.: privately printed for the author, 1941.

Arthur, John Preston. *Western North Carolina: A History from 1730 to 1913*. Johnson City, TN: Overmountain Press, 1996.

Brewer, Carson, and Alberta Brewer. *Valley So Wild*. Knoxville: East Tennessee Historical Society, 1975.

Broome, Harvey. *Out Under the Sky of the Great Smokies*. Knoxville: University of Tennessee Press, 2001.

Campbell, A.G. *Hunting the Wild Boar and Bear of Appalachia*. Tabor City, NC: Atlantic Publishing Company, 1985.

Casada, Jim. *Fly Fishing in the Great Smoky Mountains National Park*. Boone, NC: High Country Press, 2009.

Coggins, Allen R. *Place Names of the Smokies*. Gatlinburg, TN: Great Smoky Mountains Natural History Association, 1999.

Crow, Vernon H. *Storm in the Mountains*. Cherokee, NC: Press of the Museum of the Cherokee Indian, 1982.

Davis, Donald Edward. *Where There Are Mountains*. Athens: University of Georgia Press, 2000.

Duncan, Barbara R., with Brett Riggs. *Cherokee Heritage Trails Guidebook*. Chapel Hill: University of North Carolina Press, 2003.

Dyer, Jerry. "A Carolina Bred Hound." *Carolina Outdoors*, February 1972.

Dykeman, Wilma. *The French Broad*. New York: Rhinehart, 1955.

Ellison, George. *Mountain Passages: Natural and Cultural History of Western North Carolina and the Great Smoky Mountains*. Charleston, SC: The History Press, 2005.

Emerson, William. "Cold Noses and Bears." *Newsweek*, December 14, 1953.

Frome, Michael. *Strangers in High Places*. Knoxville: University of Tennessee Press, 1966.

Fulton, Patti S. *Let the Record Show*. Franklin, TN: Hillsboro Press, 2001.

Gasque, Jim. *Hunting and Fishing in the Great Smokies*. New York: Alfred A. Knopf, 1948.

Gotbold-Russell. *Confederate Colonel and Cherokee Chief*. Knoxville: University of Tennessee Press, 1990.

Hart, William D., Jr. *3,000 Miles in the Great Smokies*. Charleston, SC: The History Press, 2009.

Holland, Lance. *Fontana: A Pocket History of Appalachia*. Robbinsville, NC: privately printed for the author, 2001.

Hunnicutt, Samuel, J. *Twenty Years Hunting and Fishing in the Great Smoky Mountains*. Maryville, TN: Byron's Publishers, 1951.

Kephart, Horace. *Our Southern Highlanders*. Reprint, Knoxville: University of Tennessee Press, 1976.

Knap, Jerome. "The Plott Hound—Tough Cookie for a Tough Job." *Hunting Magazine* (May 1975).

Legare, Robert. "Plott Dogs." *Outdoorsman Magazine* (January 1944).

Maloney, John. "The Hounds of Plott Valley." *True Magazine* (November 1951).

Mason, Robert. *Lure of the Great Smokies*. Boston: Houghton Mifflin Company, 1927.

McClung, Marshall. *More Mountain People, Places and Things*. Robbinsville, NC: Graham County Historical Association, 2011.

———. *Mountain People, Places and Things*. Robbinsville, NC: Graham County Historical Association, 2006.

Methven, Frank T. *The Sound of the Hills*. Pittsburgh, PA: Dorrance Publishing Company, 2006.

Moss, Bill. *The Westfieldts of Ruby Grange*. United States: Whitney Press Inc., 2013.

National Plott Hound Association. *1959 Year Book*. N.p.: self-published, 1959.

Oliver, Duane. *Hazel Creek: From Then Until Now*. United States: privately published by the author, 1989.

Parris, John. *Mountain Bred*. Raleigh, NC: Edwards and Broughton Company, 1967.

———. *Roaming the Mountains*. Raleigh, NC: Edwards and Broughton Company, 1955.

———. *These Storied Mountains*. Raleigh, NC: Edwards and Broughton Company, 1972.

Pierce, Daniel. *The Great Smokies: From Natural Habitat to National Park*. Knoxville: University of Tennessee Press, 2000.

Plott, Bob. *Colorful Characters of the Great Smoky Mountains*. Charleston, SC: The History Press, 2011.

———. *A History of Hunting in the Great Smoky Mountains*. Charleston, SC: The History Press, 2008.

———. *Legendary Hunters of the Southern Highlands*. Charleston, SC: The History Press, 2009.

———. *Strike and Stay: The Story of the Plott Hound*. Charleston, SC: The History Press, 2007.

Powell, William. *The North Carolina Gazetteer*. Chapel Hill: University of North Carolina Press, 1968.

Robinson, Jerome. "The Most Prized Big Game Dog in the World." *Sports Afield* (April 1973).

Rose, Major Don. *Quill*. Raleigh, NC: Ivy House Publishing, 2003.

Rozema, Vicki. *Footsteps of the Cherokee*. Winston Salem, NC: John Blair Publishing, 1995.

Strutin, Michael. *History Hikes of the Great Smokies*. Gatlinburg, TN: Great Smoky Mountains Natural History Association, 2003.

Swain County Genealogical and Historical Society. *History of Swain County*. Winston Salem, NC: Hunter Publishing, 1988. Includes various articles by George Ellison, Lee Woods, Helen Cable Vance, Lula Allen Cable and Anne Ballew.

Thomsen, Paul. *Rebel Chief*. New York: Tom Doherty and Associates, 2004.

Trout, Ed. *Historic Buildings of the Great Smokies*. Gatlinburg, TN: Great Smoky Mountains Natural History Association, 1995.

Wiggonton, Elliott. *Foxfire Five*. Garden City, NY: Anchor Books, 1979.

Williams, Michael Ann. *Great Smoky Mountain Folklife*. Jackson: University of Mississippi Press, 1995.

Wise, Ken. *Hiking Trails of the Great Smoky Mountains*. 2nd ed. Knoxville: University of Tennessee Press, 2104.

Zeigler, Wilbur, and Ben Grosscup. *Heart of the Alleghenies*. Raleigh, NC: Alfred Williams, 1883.

ABOUT THE AUTHOR

Bob Plott is a third great-grandson of (Johannes) George Plott, who first brought the Plott bear hounds to America in the mid-eighteenth century, and he is a great-great-nephew of Henry Plott, who introduced the breed to the Great Smoky Mountains in the early 1800s.

He has spent most of his professional life working as either a manufacturing executive or a martial arts instructor, although for the last ten years he has been employed in the NASCAR racing industry.

Bob is the author of four other award-winning books—*Strike and Stay: The Story of the Plott Hound* (2007), *A History of Hunting in the Great Smoky Mountains* (2008), *Legendary Hunters of the Southern Highlands* (2009) and *Colorful Characters of the Great Smoky Mountains* (2011)—all published by The History Press. He has written monthly magazine articles for three national hunting magazines for the past decade, as well as multiple free-lance columns for publications such as *Wildlife in North Carolina*, *Smoky Mountain Living*, the *AKC Gazette* and *Carolina Country*, among many others.

Plott is also member of the esteemed speaker's roster for the North Carolina Humanities Council's Roads Scholar Program and has conducted historical programs for them across the Southeast. He has also been featured on *UNC Public Television*, the weekly nationally syndicated television show *Life in the Carolinas*, the History Channel television show *Only in America*, *National Public Radio* and the nationally syndicated *John Boy and Billy Radio Big Show*.

In 2009, Plott and his friend David Brewin were advisors for the Western Carolina University Plott Hound museum exhibit at the Mountain Heritage

Center. The award-winning exhibit continues to tour extensively across the Southeast. Later that same year, Bob provided Plott hounds and served as technical advisor for the movie *The World Made Straight*, based on the novel of the same name by Ron Rash.

Plott is one of the founding members of PlottFest, a two-day festival held annually in Maggie Valley, North Carolina, celebrating the Plott breed and southern mountain culture. Over the past four years, PlottFest has raised more than $100,000 for local charities.

In 2016, Bob was awarded the Order of the Longleaf Pine by the governor of North Carolina. It is the most prestigious award given to civilian citizens of the Tar Heel State. Previous winners include, among others, Doc Watson, Balsam Range, Billy Graham and Andy Griffith.

Bob was recently added to the *Traditional Artists Directory of the Blue Ridge National Heritage Area*. He and his family continue to raise the family Plott hounds at their Plott Ridge Kennels, near Eufola, North Carolina. Visit his website at www.bobplott.com.

Also by Bob Plott:

Strike and Stay: The Story of the Plott Hound

A History of Hunting in the Great Smoky Mountains

Legendary Hunters of the Southern Highlands

Colorful Characters of the Great Smoky Mountains